# EMPOWERED

## CHOOSING TO LIVE BY THE POWER OF THE HOLY SPIRIT

**DALE EVRIST & JOEL EVRIST**

CORE4
SERIES

Printed in the United States of America.
ISBN - 9781081378370

# TABLE OF CONTENTS

# INTRODUCTION

---

In Jesus' earthly ministry, He said and did everything by the will of God the Father and the work of the Holy Spirit. It was the person and power of the Holy Spirit that led Him on and anointed and empowered all that He said and did. He accomplished the divine plan of God through the divine power of the Holy Spirit. He commanded His disciples to do the very same thing in order to fulfill His divine mission for them to share His love and power with everyone, everywhere. And so, this is true of all followers of Jesus for all times. The will of God and the work of the Holy Spirit—the person and power of the Holy Spirit—is what must lead us on and anoint and empower everything we say and do.

*Empowered* is a Bible-study handbook for everyone desiring to learn how to follow Jesus' example of obeying the will of God the Father in everything by the truth of the Word and the person and power of the Holy Spirit. This resource will help equip you to live a Spirit-empowered life that will have a dynamic and dramatic impact on your life and the lives of all you touch. Discover the secret of the Savior's success and how to unlock that secret to see it be on open display. Living a Spirit-empowered life will change you forever.

In this resource, you will engage with and go through 12 lessons that will help you learn how to live by the power of the Holy Spirit in everything at all times by focusing on:

1. LIVING BY THE POWER OF THE HOLY SPIRIT: THE WAY CHOSEN FOR YOU

2. THE POWER OF THE BAPTISM AND FILLING WITH THE HOLY SPIRIT

3. THE POWER OF THE HOLY SPIRIT IN THE WORD

4. THE POWER OF THE HOLY SPIRIT IN PRAYER

5. THE POWER OF THE HOLY SPIRIT IN PRAISE

6. THE POWER OF THE HOLY SPIRIT'S GIFTS, PART 1

7. THE POWER OF THE HOLY SPIRIT'S GIFTS, PART 2

8. THE POWER OF THE HOLY SPIRIT'S FRUIT, PART 1

9. THE POWER OF THE HOLY SPIRIT'S FRUIT, PART 2

10. THE POWER OF THE HOLY SPIRIT'S SANCTIFICATION, PART 1

11. THE POWER OF THE HOLY SPIRIT'S SANCTIFICATION. PART 2

12. LIVING BY THE POWER OF THE HOLY SPIRIT: THE CHOICE IS NOW YOURS

In each lesson, you will find the following features to help guide you on your journey of learning to live every day by the power of the Holy Spirit:

## Scriptures and Checkboxes

*Empowered* is filled with scriptures to be read and understood. The checkbox (❑) next to the reference is meant to be marked off as each one is read. This will help you to not miss any of the biblical references as well as serve as an encouragement that you are familiarizing yourself more and more with God's Word.

## Lesson Introduction

Each lesson begins with some introductory thoughts on the lesson's theme. These will help you as a pursuer of the person and power of the Holy Spirit to prepare your heart and mind to fully engage with the subject matter.

## Lesson Definition

These are clear and concise definitions of the words that make up the focus of each lesson and how they are used in the Bible. Understanding what these words mean in the languages the Scriptures were written will give you needed clarity for responding fully to the truths found in the lesson.

## Memorize

As a part of each lesson, there is a scripture to memorize and meditate on. This will help the truths communicated go deeper and be applied more dynamically in your life.

## Key Truth

Much like the scripture to be memorized, there is a key truth that reinforces the primary focus of the lesson. This helps to more deeply "drive home" its theme.

## Your Response

This part of each lesson helps you answer the question, "Now what?" Here you will find steps of practical application that will make living by the power of the Holy Spirit an encouraging, enriching, and effective reality.

## Written Response: Lesson Review

By writing out certain parts of each lesson, you will be helped to review key sentences and statements and reinforce their truths in your life.

## Written Response: Life Reflection

This part of each lesson will help you reflect on what you have learned and how you will apply that in your life. You will be provided prompts to help you journal your journey as a Spirit-empowered follower of Jesus.

## GOING THROUGH EMPOWERED

You can certainly go through *Empowered* on your own and gain significant growth in your pursuit of living by the power of the Holy Spirit. However, the most effective way to use this resource is to be guided through the process by another disciple who is more mature in living by the power of the Holy Spirit than you are. Thoroughly working through the lesson on your own and then having a regular discipleship meeting with someone committed to Spirit-empowered living will produce even deeper and more dynamic results.

## TAKING SOMEONE THROUGH EMPOWERED

After going through *Empowered* yourself, you will be ready to make an ongoing commitment to take others through this resource as well. If seeing souls saved and disciples made is to be our main priority and passion in this life, then we need to engage this passion and practice regularly. Ask the Holy Spirit to lead you to those whom the Lord has called you to help become Spirit-empowered followers of Jesus. Set up regular discipleship meetings and have those you are discipling come into those meetings having thoroughly gone through the lesson you are covering. Your preparation will be reviewing the lesson, praying for the discipleship meeting and trusting the Holy Spirit to guide and grace every part.

*The most important work you will ever do is helping people of all ages and stages to become faithful, fruitful, Spirit-empowered followers of Jesus.*

# LIVING BY THE POWER OF THE HOLY SPIRIT: THE WAY CHOSEN FOR YOU

## INTRODUCTION

❏ *Read Galatians 5:16-25*

Living by the leading and power of the Holy Spirit enables us to live a life of fellowship, fullness and freedom. Once we are saved and baptized and filled with the Holy Spirit, we must then learn how to abide in the Spirit moment by moment and day by day. We are not called to ever live or minister in our own strength but always in the power and strength of God's Spirit. The Holy Spirit desires to be our constant companion and helper, leading us into the will of God the Father and Jesus the Son and giving us the spiritual guidance and strength to see it come to pass. When God's people were rebuilding the temple in Jerusalem, God told them through the prophet Zechariah that the only way to complete this heavenly task was by the work and the power of God's Spirit. (❏ Read Zechariah 4:6-9.) Jesus told His disciples that apart from the work of His Spirit as they abided in Him they would not be able to accomplish anything of any eternal worth. (❏ Read John 14:26; John 15:4-5.) Having started our life

*Having started our life and ministry in Christ by the work of the Spirit we must continue to live by the Spirit, seeing Christ's plans for us fulfilled completely as we embrace the walk, the way, and the work in and of the Spirit.*

and ministry in Christ by the work of the Spirit we must continue to live by the Spirit, seeing Christ's plans for us fulfilled completely as we embrace the walk, the way, and the work in and of the Spirit.

## THE WALK IN THE SPIRIT

Walking in the Spirit involves submitting to the *person, purpose and power* of the Holy Spirit. The Holy Spirit is the presence of the Father and the Son in us, helping and guiding us to discover the Father's and the Son's will and purpose by divine wisdom and power. (❏ Read John 14:16; 15:26; 1 John 4:4.) Walking in the Holy Spirit is a partnership between the Holy Spirit and us. We yield to Him in faith and obedience and He supplies everything we need to be fruitful believers and ministers. He leads us as we study God's Word, giving us revelation and insight—eternal truth

*Walking in the Spirit involves submitting to the person, purpose and power of the Holy Spirit.*

to learn from and live by. (❏ Read John 16:13-15.) He helps us in our human weaknesses to know how to pray and what to pray. (❏ Read Romans 8:26-27.) Paul told the Ephesian church that they would understand the power of this kind of living. In so doing they would find themselves strengthened by the mighty power of the Holy Spirit in them, rooted and grounded, full and satisfied in the love of

*Notes*

Christ and the knowledge of His will for them.
(❑ Read Ephesians 3:14-21.)

It is no wonder we are called to "Walk in the Spirit."
(❑ Read Romans 8:1-4.) It is the only truly wise and wonderful way to live. By walking in the Spirit, we partner with the Lord Jesus in what He is doing around the corner and around the world, across the street and across the waters. Our eyes are opened to see what He intends to do in our lives and times and how He intends on accomplishing it by His Spirit.

## THE WAY OF THE SPIRIT

The way of the Spirit is about a new kind of living. It is the way of abundant and glorious liberty. (❑ Read John 10:10; Romans 7:4-6.) The Holy Spirit desires to set us free from trying to do what is spiritually right in our own strength. He comes to set us free from the penalty, power, guilt and shame of sin. Sin no longer has dominion over us.
(❑ Read Romans 6:11-14.) We are now free to serve and obey God on His terms according to the truth and direction of His Word and the leading and life of His Spirit. As we abide in Him and trust His strength, we have the supernatural ability to live for Jesus and obey

*The Holy Spirit desires to set us free from trying to do what is spiritually right in our own strength.*

Him in everything. This provides us with a life of high purpose and deep and abiding joy.

## THE WORK OF THE SPIRIT

The work that the Holy Spirit desires to accomplish in us is a work of *purity, passion and power*. Remember, He is called the *Holy Spirit*. He brings the purity of God's presence and character into our lives so that we can receive and reflect the glory of His holiness in the earth. (❏ Read 1 Peter 1:16.) This is not self-righteousness. In fact, it is the very opposite; it is the very righteousness of Christ, received and released in us and through us by His Spirit.

*God in us by the Holy Spirit has come to see the full work of salvation in spirit, soul and body become a blessed reality.*

The Spirit also produces in us a deep, abiding passion to love Jesus supremely and seek to please Him everything. Paul told the Philippians that both the desire to fulfill God's will and the dynamic power to fulfill His will was the result of God's Spirit living within us. (❏ Read Philippians 2:12-13.) God in us by the Holy Spirit has come to see the full work of salvation in spirit, soul and body become a blessed reality. This work in us then becomes the work through us that touches and transforms every life we encounter.

*Notes*

Consider the following truths concerning the work of the Holy Spirit in us:

- He makes us spiritually new. (❑ Read Titus 3:5.)

- He fills and empowers us to minister the life of Jesus. (❑ Read Acts 2:33.)

- He is the presence of the Father and the Son in us. (❑ Read John 14:15-18.)

- He produces the fruit of godly life and character in us. (❑ Read Galatians 5:22-23.)

- He leads and guides us into the perfect will of God on a daily basis. (❑ Read John 16:13-14.)

- He satisfies the deepest needs of our lives. (❑ Read John 7:37-39.)

- He fills us with the love of God. (❑ Read Romans 5:5.)

- He gives us supernatural gifts and abilities. (❑ Read 1 Corinthians 12:11.)

- He helps us pray with precision and power. (❑ Read Romans 8:26-28.)

- He opens our eyes to understand spiritual things. (❑ Read 1 Corinthians 2:9-16.)

- He produces unity with other believers, so we can live in peace and love. (❑ Read Ephesians 4:3-4.)

- He supplies the breakthrough power of the kingdom of God to overcome all the power of the kingdom of demonic darkness.
  (❏ Read Matthew 12:28.)

According to the Scriptures, living by the power of the Holy Spirit is the way chosen for you by God the Father and Jesus the Son. If you will say yes to God's way, you will find that living by the person and the power of the Holy Spirit in everything is the most fulfilling and exciting way to spend the days, months and years of one's lifetime. Engaging in this way of living will provide a life truly worth living.

*According to the Scriptures, living by the power of the Holy Spirit is the way chosen for you by God the Father and Jesus the Son.*

MEMORIZE: *"If we live in the Spirit, let us also walk in the Spirit."* (Galatians 5:25)

Use the following lines to write out the scripture to help you commit it to memory.

_____

_____

_____

_____

_____

_____

_____

KEY TRUTH: Living by the leading and the power of the Holy Spirit enables us to live with fellowship, fullness and freedom.

## YOUR RESPONSE:

This is how you can choose to live by the power of the Holy Spirit as you apply the truths from this lesson to your life.

- Ask the Holy Spirit to reveal any area of your life where you have not fully submitted to Him, His purpose, and His power.

- Ask the Holy Spirit to reveal any area of your life where you are relying on your own strength instead of Him.

- Ask the Holy Spirit to reveal any area of your life where you are not allowing Him to work in you and through you.

- Take time to repent in the areas revealed to you above and make a fresh commitment to live by the power of the Holy Spirit each and every day.

## WRITTEN RESPONSE: LESSON REVIEW

Review each section from the lesson on the previous pages to fill in each blank below. This review will help to reinforce the truths from this lesson in your life.

1. Living by the _____ and _____ of the Holy Spirit _____ us to live a life of _____, _____ and _____.

2. Having started our _____ and _____ in Christ by the _____ of the Spirit we must continue to _____ by the Spirit, seeing Christ's _____ for us _____ completely as we embrace the _____, the _____, and the _____ in and of the Spirit.

3. _____ in the Spirit involves _____ to the _____, _____ and _____ of the Holy Spirit.

4. The _____ of the Spirit is about a _____ _____ of living. It is the _____ of _____ and _____ liberty.

5. According to the Scriptures, _____ by the _____ of the Holy Spirit is the _____ chosen for _____ by God the Father and Jesus the Son.

**WRITTEN RESPONSE:** LIFE REFLECTION

Using the journaling section on the pages at the end of this lesson, write in your own words your responses to the following questions.

1.  What have you learned and what has impacted you personally from this lesson?

2.  In reading the scripture references in this lesson, what are you sensing and seeing the Holy Spirit highlight and reveal to you that will enable you to better live by the power of the Holy Spirit in everything?

3.  As a disciple choosing to live by the power of the Holy Spirit, what steps of faith-filled obedience do you need to take to see what you have learned in this lesson become ongoing practices and patterns in your life?

*Journal*

*Journal*

# THE POWER OF THE BAPTISM AND FILLING WITH THE HOLY SPIRIT

## INTRODUCTION

❏ *Read Acts 1:8; Ephesians 5:18*

Jesus wants to baptize and fill you with the person and power of the Holy Spirit to make you an effective witness for Him to everyone, everywhere. Just before Jesus was taken up into heaven, He told His disciples two very important things. The first was that they were called and commissioned to preach the gospel to everyone, everywhere and make disciples of all those who believed. (❏ Read Matthew 28:19; Mark 16:15.) The second was that they were to wait in Jerusalem until they were baptized and filled with the power of the Holy Spirit. (❏ Read Luke 24:49.) In essence Jesus was saying, "until you're baptized and filled with Holy Spirit, don't go! After you're baptized and filled with the Holy Spirit, don't stay!" So, let's learn what it means to truly be *appointed* and *anointed* by Jesus our Lord through the person and power of the Holy Spirit.

*Jesus wants to baptize and fill you with the person and power of the Holy Spirit to make you an effective witness for Him to everyone, everywhere.*

## THE PERSON OF HOLY SPIRIT BAPTISM AND FILLING: JESUS

Jesus is the One who baptizes and fills you with the person

and power of the Holy Spirit. John the Baptist said the Savior who was coming after him was the Anointed One who would anoint, baptize and fill with the Holy Spirit. (❏ Read Mark 1:8.) He is our King and He desires to empower us to be ambassadors for His kingdom wherever we go. (❏ Read 2 Corinthians 5:20.)

## THE PURPOSE OF HOLY SPIRIT BAPTISM AND FILLING: AUTHORITY AND POWER

When Jesus was still on earth He appointed, anointed and sent out His disciples. They were to go *declaring, defining and defending* the gospel of the kingdom and *demonstrating* its power by His Holy Spirit. He gave them both the legal authority to speak and act in His name, as well as the dynamic power to defeat the devil and to deliver people from his hellish influence and impact. And so it is with us today: We need King Jesus to powerfully anoint us to go forth and advance the kingdom of God over the forces of hell and into the hearts of people. Jesus told His disciples that they would receive explosive power to go and be witnesses for Him in the earth. (❏ Read Luke 9:1-6; 10:1-9.) The authority to

*The authority to use the name of Jesus and the power of Jesus to set men free from the power of sin and Satan is available to every willing and expectant believer.*

*Notes*

use the name of Jesus and the power of Jesus to set men free from the power of sin and Satan is available to every willing and expectant believer.

## THE PROCESS OF HOLY SPIRIT BAPTISM AND FILLING: ASKING AND RECEIVING IN EXPECTANT FAITH

As stated earlier, Jesus had instructed His followers to wait until they received the power of the Holy Spirit they needed. One hundred and twenty obedient followers assembled in an upper room of a house in Jerusalem. For ten days they worshiped, prayed, fellowshipped and waited for what Jesus had promised them. They believed what He had said to them. They loved Him passionately and desired to have everything they needed to remain close to Him and share Him with others. They expected to receive the empowering

*If we earnestly desire to be anointed by Jesus, our King, He will pour out His Spirit on and into our lives.*

and filling of the Holy Spirit because they trusted Him and took Him at His word. God rewarded their expectant faith when, on the Day of Pentecost, the power and filling of the Holy Spirit came. They experienced the sound of a powerful wind. Tongues of fire appeared over each person's head. They spoke in languages they had never learned and poured out into the streets with powerful preaching that drew 3,000 people to Christ. All of this was the work of the Holy Spirit. (❏ Read Acts 1 and 2.)

We, too, will receive the baptism and filling with the Holy Spirit when we ask in passionate faith. If we earnestly desire to be anointed by Jesus, our King, He will pour out His Spirit on and into our lives. If we ask Him for the baptism and filling with the Holy Spirit, He will not deny us. (❏ Read Luke 11:13.) The following are some of the results in the lives of the disciples being baptized and filled with the Holy Spirit. These will be evident in our lives as well when we allow Jesus to baptize and fill us with the Holy Spirit.

- The release of passionate faith

- Prayerful expectation

- Full place given to the Holy Spirit

- The baptism and filling with the Holy Spirit

- Supernatural manifestations

- Powerful witness for Christ

- Significant spiritual fruitfulness

## THE PROOFS OF HOLY SPIRIT BAPTISM AND FILLING: PROCLAMATION AND POWER

After we are baptized and filled with the Holy Spirit, we need to stay filled by giving ourselves to prayer, worship, growing in the Word and ministering to others. (❑ Read Ephesians 5:18-20.) We also should help others experience the baptism and filling with the Holy Spirit and encourage them in daily Spirit-filled living. We can confidently expect these signs in our lives when we are baptized and filled with His Spirit:

- **An anointing with dynamic power.**
  (❑ Read Acts 4:1-6.) Jesus told His disciples that they would be clothed with power from heaven. (❑ Read Luke 24:49.) So, one of the proofs of being baptized and filled with the Holy Spirit is that we are anointed with the power of Jesus Christ to do His works. We, too, are called and equipped to heal the sick, hear God's voice and follow His direction. We are also anointed to cast out demons and defeat the schemes of the devil. Powerless Christianity will produce very little to advance Christ's kingdom and fulfill Christ's Great Commission. But people who know Jesus intimately and are anointed by him powerfully will be used to carry on and carry out the mission He was called to. (❑ Read Luke 4:18-19.)

- **The release of spiritual language.**
(❏ Read Acts 2:4; 10:44-47; 19:6.) Another
resource available to Spirit-filled believers is
a spiritual language given by the Holy Spirit.
Spiritual language or "tongues" is given for
personal edification, expanded prayer beyond our
human ability, expanded praise and worship, and a
divine message that edifies the church and is a sign
to unbelievers. (❏ Read 1 Corinthians 14.)

- **Increased courage and boldness.** Another
sign of the Spirit's fullness is a supernatural
confidence to face whatever challenges, threats or
hardships that come our way. Peter and John were
threatened by religious leaders for preaching in
Jesus' name. Their companions prayed for them
and they were filled with holy boldness. They
continued preaching and ministering to others in
the power of the Holy Spirit. (❏ Read Acts 4:1-31.)

- **Evangelistic passion.** After Saul of Tarsus was
saved, baptized and filled with the Holy Spirit, he
preached the gospel with a passion to see Jesus
exalted and people come to faith in Him.
(❏ Read Acts 9:17-22.) People who are truly
baptized and filled with the Holy Spirit will seek to
see souls saved with great zeal.

*Notes*

- **The release and overflow of praise, worship and thanksgiving.** When someone is truly baptized and filled with the Holy Spirit, they will sing and shout for joy in the Lord. A "river" of gratitude and praise will flow freely from the hearts of those who are led by the Holy Spirit to declare the grace and greatness of God the Father and Jesus Christ, His Son. (❑ Read Ephesians 5:18-20.)

## THE PROGRESS OF HOLY SPIRIT BAPTISM AND FILLING: RECEIVING DAILY, FRESH FILLINGS

As Spirit-filled believers, we are called to one baptism then daily and seasonal fresh, new and deeper fillings. The Holy Spirit is always wanting to increase our spiritual capacity to face new challenges and to lay hold of new levels of impact and effectiveness. (❑ Read Acts 4.) We are called to seek to be filled with the Holy Spirit freshly and daily. We are called to be open to the Spirit increasing our spiritual capacity in every new season of life and ministry. When we do this, we can expect dynamic spiritual growth as an ongoing work of the Holy Spirit in our lives.

*As Spirit-filled believers, we are called to one baptism then daily and seasonal fresh, new and deeper fillings.*

MEMORIZE: *"And do not be drunk with wine, in which is dissipation; but be filled with the Spirit,"* (Ephesians 5:18)

Use the following lines to write out the scripture to help you commit it to memory.

_____

_____

_____

_____

_____

_____

KEY TRUTH: Jesus wants to fill you with the person and power of the Holy Spirit to make you an effective witness for Him in the world.

## YOUR RESPONSE:

This is how you can choose to live by the power of the Holy Spirit as you apply the truths from this lesson to your life.

- Every day ask the Holy Spirit for a fresh filling for your life.

- Walk and work in and by the Holy Spirit's power in every encounter of every day.

- Lead others to be baptized and filled with the Holy Spirit and to be led and empowered by Him daily.

- As you journal, keep a careful record of your increased spiritual capacity and growth in every new season of your life and ministry.

## WRITTEN RESPONSE: LESSON REVIEW

Review each section from the lesson on the previous pages to fill in each blank below. This review will help to reinforce the truths from this lesson in your life.

1. Jesus is the One who _____ and _____
   you with the _____ and _____ of the
   Holy Spirit.

2. We need King Jesus to _____ _____
   us to go forth and _____ the _____ of
   God over the forces of _____ and into the hearts of
   _____.

3. If we earnestly _____ to be _____
   by Jesus, our King, He will _____ out His Spirit
   _____ and _____ our lives.

4. After we are _____ and _____ with
   the Holy Spirit, we need to _____ filled by
   giving ourselves to _____, _____,
   _____ in the Word and _____ to others.

5. As Spirit-filled _____ we are called to
   _____ baptism, then _____ and
   _____ fresh, new and deeper _____.

## WRITTEN RESPONSE: LIFE REFLECTION

Using the journaling section on the pages at the end of this lesson, write in your own words your responses to the following questions.

1.  What have you learned and what has impacted you personally from this lesson?

2.  In reading the scripture references in this lesson, what are you sensing and seeing the Holy Spirit highlight and reveal to you that will enable you to better live by the power of the Holy Spirit in everything?

3.  As a disciple choosing to live by the power of the Holy Spirit, what steps of faith-filled obedience do you need to take to see what you have learned in this lesson become ongoing practices and patterns in your life?

*Journal*

*Journal*

*Journal*

# LESSON 3

## THE POWER OF THE HOLY SPIRIT IN THE WORD

*Notes*

## INTRODUCTION

❏ *Read John 14:26; 16:13-15; 2 Timothy 3:16-17; 2 Peter 1:20-21*

The Apostle John declared Jesus to be the Living Word of God. (❏ Read John 1:1-14; Revelation 19:13.) The Apostle Paul declared that all that must be known about the godhead has been manifest in bodily form in Jesus Christ. (❏ Read Colossians 2:9.) Jesus is the living and complete description of the godhead. In harmony with the Living Word of God, Jesus Himself attested to the power and revelation of the Scriptures – the written Word of God. Jesus said that the written Word revealed God the Father's character and plan and bore witness to Jesus as Messiah. (❏ Read Matthew 5:43-48; John 5:39.)

The writers of the Old and New Testaments declare that the written Word of God is living, active, powerful, fully tested and purified, unchanging, altogether righteous, able to convert the soul, make wise the simple, cause

*The study and application of the written Word of God is a preeminent priority for any true disciple of the Living Word of God.*

blessing and fruitfulness, cleanse a person's life, renew a person's mind, refocus a person's faith in the midst of trial, and thoroughly equip a man or woman of God for every good work. (❏ Read Psalm 1:2-3; 19:7-10; 119:9-11;

2 Timothy 3:16-17; Hebrews 4:12.) The study and application of the written Word of God is a preeminent priority for any true disciple of the Living Word of God. Here is an important key: the written Word was inspired by the Holy Spirit through faithful scribes and thus can only be understood by the Holy Spirit to faithful students. We need the Spirit's power to understand and appropriately respond to the Word He inspired, and to teach us all things.

## INVESTIGATION OF THE WORD

Investigation is about discovering what the Word of God *says*. In this, we do the work necessary to enable us to truly see what is there in the text. The writer of Hebrews says that God is a rewarder of those who *diligently seek* Him. (❏ Read Hebrews 11:6.) The words diligently seek in the original language have to do with intense investigation, inquiry, and scrutiny of a subject. How can we effectively investigate and accurately represent a God who is infinite in wisdom, power and glory? The prophet Isaiah tells us that when the Holy Spirit rests on a person, He gives that person wisdom, understanding, counsel, might, knowledge, and the revelation of how to fear the LORD. (❏ Read Isaiah 11:2.) This Spirit rested on Jesus, which is why people were so astonished at His understanding of the Scriptures in the absence of the formal training of the day. (❏ Read John 7:15-18.)

*Notes*

Jesus tells His disciples that when the Helper, the Holy Spirit, comes, He will teach them all things. (❑ Read John 14:26.) Before the empowerment of the Holy Spirit, the apostles were greatly limited in their ability to investigate and understand the Scriptures. Jesus, by the power of the Holy Spirit, unfolded everything the Scriptures said concerning His messiahship. (❑ Read Luke 24:27; 44-48.) Yet, the apostles still didn't fully understand. But once Pentecost had come, the Spirit who inspired the written Word of God instilled power and wisdom into the apostles to accurately investigate God in the Scriptures and accurately communicate God's plan to the people. (❑ Read Acts 2:14-39; 3:12-26; 4:23-30.) The apostles' doctrine was born out of the Holy Spirit's anointing. (❑ Read Acts 2:42.)

All investigation of the Scriptures must begin with asking and earnestly desiring a fresh filling of the Spirit's power, knowledge, wisdom and instruction. He faithfully revealed, protected and preserved the Scriptures through the disciples of old, and He is faithful to do the same through all faithful disciples for all time.

*Investigation is about discovering what the Word of God says.*

## INTERPRETATION OF THE WORD

Interpretation is about discovering what the Word

of God *means*. There is practical work for us to do to understand what the writer meant by the words he used to communicate to his audience. The Apostle Peter wrote that the Scriptures were written by men moved by the Holy Spirit. (❑ Read 2 Peter 1:20-21.) The words *moved by* in the original language denote the idea of having something laid upon you by another or given to you by another. The authors of the Scriptures received the Word and its meaning from the Holy Spirit – not themselves. We too need the Holy Spirit to give to us the interpretation of the Scriptures through His empowerment and teaching.

*Interpretation is about discovering what the Word of God means.*

In a moment of sorrow as His disciples anticipated the coming departure of their Rabbi, Jesus told them that the Holy Spirit, their soon-coming Helper, would be just like their Lord. (❑ Read John 14:16.) As Jesus opened the understanding of His disciples to comprehend the meaning of the Scriptures, so the Holy Spirit does for us. (❑ Read Luke 24:45.) Spirit-empowered investigation is about knowing where to dig and what to learn in the *goldmine* of God's Word. Spirit-empowered interpretation is about being taught by the Spirit to understand what the text means and what it requires of the reader.

## MEDITATION ON THE WORD

Meditation is about discovering how the Word of God *transforms*. In Psalms we discover that meditation transforms a person's life into a state of constant fruitfulness and blessing. (❑ Read Psalm 1:2-3.) David said that meditation on God's Word converts (or restores) a person's soul, makes the simple-minded wise, causes the heart to rejoice, and enlightens a person's perspective on the pure meaning of life. (❑ Read Psalm 19:7-8.) We also learn that when the Word of God is hidden in a heart, it produces a life that strives against sin for righteousness. (❑ Read Psalm 119:11.)

Followers of Jesus are called to meditate on the Word like He did. How was Jesus able to quote verses, passages, and entire chapters of Scripture at will? First, He was led by the Spirit concerning what verses to hide in His heart. Second, the Spirit brought to His mind what verses the Father wanted Him to exclaim and explain to the people. (❑ Read John 5:19, 30; 7:16.) The word *meditation* in the Old Testament is likened to a cow chewing a cud until it can be swallowed, digested, and used for energy. The Scriptures cannot be fully understood nor have their full transforming work in a person's life unless they are deeply mulling them over with the power

> *Meditation is about discovering how the Word of God transforms.*

of the Holy Spirit. The Apostle James had been led by the
Spirit to memorize a passage in the book of Amos, and as
he meditated on these verses the Spirit transformed his
understanding of God's plan of salvation for the Gentiles.
(❏ Read Amos 9:11-12; Acts 15:13-21.)

The Holy Spirit knows what verses and passages we need
to memorize and meditate on so that He can transform
us through the renewing of our minds. The power of the
Spirit in the Word isn't just about daily investigation
and interpretation, but a journey of Spirit-led, Spirit-
empowered memorization and meditation. Jesus said the
Spirit would take what the Father wills and the Son wills
and declare to us. (❏ Read John 16:14-15.) Let us ask the
Holy Spirit to show us how the Father and the Son desire
to transform us through the Word every day.

## APPLICATION OF THE WORD

Application is about discovering what the Word of God
*requires*. The Apostle James teaches his readers that they
must be doers of the Word. (❏ Read James 1:22.) Jesus
told His disciples that knowing His Word wasn't enough,
but that full blessing comes from doing the Word. (❏ Read
John 13:17.) The problem arises when a disciple of Jesus
attempts to obey and apply the Word of God in their own
strength and by their own wisdom. This is a key problem
the Apostle Paul addresses in the church of Galatia. The
church had turned from a grace-based, Spirit-led liberty

in following Christ to an attempt to achieve righteousness through the human efforts of the Law. Paul explained that no man can be righteous before God through human effort. Only those who walk (or live) in and by the power and wisdom of the Holy Spirit can live a life of freedom and obedience to Christ. (❏ Read Galatians 5:1-25.)

*Application is about discovering what the Word of God requires.*

In his pursuit to lovingly obey Jesus, the Apostle Paul realized that the law of the Spirit of life was the only way to conquer the law of sin and death warring in his flesh. (❏ Read Romans 8:1-2.) The Spirit of God shows us what the Word of God requires of us. Then, the Spirit of God provides the power and wisdom to respond. Put another way, what the Word of God demands, the Spirit of God supplies.

Every Spirit-infused desire to respond to the Word of God should be accompanied by prayers for empowering grace. He is the Spirit of truth who guides us into all truth. He doesn't just guide us *to* truth; but *into* truth. (❏ Read John 16:13.) He illuminates what the Scriptures require and imparts the spiritual resources we need to respond.

MEMORIZE: *"All Scripture is given by inspiration of God, and is profitable for doctrine, for reproof, for correction, for instruction in righteousness, that the man of God may be complete, thoroughly equipped for every good work."* (2 Timothy 3:16-17)

Use the following lines to write out the scripture to help you commit it to memory.

_____

_____

_____

_____

_____

_____

_____

KEY TRUTH: The written Word was inspired by the Holy Spirit through faithful scribes and can thus only be understood by the Holy Spirit to faithful students.

## YOUR RESPONSE:

This is how you can choose to live by the power of the Holy Spirit as you apply the truths from this lesson to your life.

- Ask the Holy Spirit to teach and empower you every time you investigate the Word.

- Ask the Holy Spirit to interpret what He instructs you to investigate.

- Ask the Holy Spirit to show what He wants you to memorize and meditate on in this season.

- Ask the Holy Spirit to give you the power and wisdom to respond to what the Word requires.

## WRITTEN RESPONSE: LESSON REVIEW

Review each section from the lesson on the previous pages to fill in each blank below. This review will help to reinforce the truths from this lesson in your life.

1. We need the Spirit's _____ to _____ and appropriately _____ to the _____ He inspired, and to _____ us _____ things.

2. Investigation is about _____ what the _____ of God _____.

3. Interpretation is about _____ what the _____ of God _____.

4. Meditation is about _____ how the _____ of God _____.

5. Application is about _____ what the _____ of God _____.

**WRITTEN RESPONSE:** LIFE REFLECTION

Using the journaling section on the pages at the end of this lesson, write in your own words your responses to the following questions.

1. What have you learned and what has impacted you personally from this lesson?

2. In reading the scripture references in this lesson, what are you sensing and seeing the Holy Spirit highlight and reveal to you that will enable you to better live by the power of the Holy Spirit in everything?

3. As a disciple choosing to live by the power of the Holy Spirit, what steps of faith-filled obedience do you need to take to see what you have learned in this lesson become ongoing practices and patterns in your life?

*Journal*

*Journal*

*Journal*

# LESSON 4

# THE POWER OF THE
# HOLY SPIRIT IN PRAYER

## INTRODUCTION

❑ *Read Jude 20-21*

The Holy Spirit is the leader and guide of your life and ministry of prayer in bringing man to God and God to man. The Apostle Paul tells us that we don't know *what* we should pray for as is needed to be perfectly in line with the will and purposes of God the Father and Jesus the Lord. So, the Holy Spirit helps us in our human weaknesses as He leads us and guides us according to heaven's divine purposes. (❑ Read Romans 8:26-27.) He gives us the spiritual ability we need to pray with accuracy and effectiveness. The Holy Spirit reveals the will of God and releases the work of God as we submit to His power and pathway in prayer. Whether the need is divine knowledge and wisdom or divine power and strength, the Spirit supplies what is needed in abundance. The key to effective prayer is to discover the will of God and come into agreement with it in faith. The Holy Spirit divinely helps us to that end.

> *The Holy Spirit reveals the will of God and releases the work of God as we submit to His power and pathway in prayer*

In addition to providing spiritual leadership for our ministry of prayer, the Holy Spirit provides us with spiritual language that enables us to pray beyond our own human abilities. He equips us to

*Notes*

pray by a means which transcends human understanding, linking us to the perfect understanding of the Holy Spirit concerning the will of God. (❏ Read 1 Corinthians 14:14-15.) Praying in the understanding and in the Spirit are both by the Holy Spirit's power. This truth is indispensable to us having a vital life and ministry of prayer.

## PRAYING BY THE POWER OF THE HOLY SPIRIT IN UNDERTAKING THE WORK OF GOD

Praying is doing the work of God to see the will of God accomplished in the earth. This work is not to be undertaken and accomplished by the power of the flesh, but by the power of the Holy Spirit. Praying in the flesh is praying by the strength of human ability to give prayer its fuel and to move it forward. It is relying on human effort to accomplish a supernatural task. It is both frustrating and largely fruitless. Theologian Martyn Lloyd Jones said, "We all know what it is to feel deadness in prayer, difficulty in prayer, to be tongue-tied, with nothing to say, as it were, having to force ourselves to try. Well, to the extent that is true of us, we are not praying in the Spirit." Unfortunately, much praying is engaged in this way and becomes exhausting and deeply discouraging. This is what always results from trying to accomplish a spiritual endeavor without the enabling of the Spirit. Remember: even "positive flesh" is still flesh. But there is, praise God, an infinitely better way to pray.

Praying in and by the power of the Holy Spirit is undertaking and engaging in the work and ministry of prayer by and in the Holy Spirit—the Spirit of Life. (❑ Read Romans 8:1-2.) It is the force and the fire of the Spirit that empowers and pushes prayer forward. It is the Holy Spirit who gives our prayers "wings" as He carries them to the Father and the Son. It becomes effortless effort as we rely on and rest in the person and power of the Holy Spirit—the very Spirit of Prayer. He brings us into the warmth and the wonder of intimate fellowship with the Living God who hears and speaks and acts on man's behalf. Enjoying a living communion with God becomes something supernaturally natural by the Holy Spirit joining us in a rewarding relational union. Then pleading the promises of God with boldness and assurance in serene confidence becomes the Spirit-supplied result. This is where the person of prayer becomes the possessor of promises. And this is where prayer becomes powerful.

*Praying is doing the work of God to see the will of God accomplished in the earth.*

## PRAYING BY THE POWER OF THE HOLY SPIRIT IN UNDERSTANDING THE WILL OF GOD

If the key to effective praying is to discover the will of God and come into agreement with it by faith, then we must know how to discover the will of God. (❑ Read 1 John 5:14-15.) According to the Apostle Paul, it is the Spirit who gives us the understanding of what the will of God is. On our own, we simply have no capacity for sensing and seeing the purposes and plans of the Lord. It is the Holy Spirit who graces us to receive the revelation we need to engage in prayer that is divinely focused and fruitful. (❑ Read 1 Corinthians 12:1-11.)

## PRAYING BY THE POWER OF THE HOLY SPIRIT IN UNSHEATHING THE WORD OF GOD

The Apostle Paul taught that the Word of God was to be seen as the sword of the Spirit. (❑ Read Ephesians 6:17.) When Paul writes of the Word of God he uses the word *rhema*, which means, *a specific spoken word of God*. It is

*Praying the Word of God by the dynamic direction of the Holy Spirit will ensure that our prayers are always on target and on time.*

the Holy Spirit who enables us to understand and apply the Scriptures. And it is also the Holy Spirit who leads us to use specific spoken words from the Scriptures that are to be received and released in prayer like a sword or dagger with Spirit-led pinpoint accuracy. Praying the Word of God produces good results. Praying specific parts of the Word of God, led and empowered by the Holy

Spirit, produces great results. We are called to "unsheathe" the sword of the Spirit, which is the specific spoken Word of God, receiving and releasing words of transformational power in prayer. Praying the Word of God by the dynamic direction of the Holy Spirit will ensure that our prayers are always on target and on time.

## PRAYING BY THE POWER OF THE HOLY SPIRIT IN UNLEASHING THE WEAPONS AND WARFARE OF GOD

After having described every aspect of the armor of God that the believer is to use in combating and conquering the schemes and attacks of the devil, Paul writes that the key to their full release is prayer in and by the power of the Holy Spirit. (❏ Read Ephesians 6:10-20.) It is by faith that we appropriate the weapons of our warfare that are mighty in God. (❏ Read 2 Corinthians 10:3-5.) And it is by Spirit-led and Spirit-empowered prayer that we activate these weapons of warfare to stand strong against the onslaught of the demonic and to resist and overcome them in all of their hellish schemes. Paul says that it is in always

*May we be found everyday rising in faith-filled, Spirit-yielded and Spirit-empowered prayer to see the Word and the will of God revealed and released in all of its liberating life and power.*

praying in all prayer and supplication in the Spirit that we resist Satan and release spiritual provision and protection for the saints. May we be found everyday rising in faith-filled, Spirit-yielded and Spirit-empowered prayer to see the Word and the will of God revealed and released in all of its liberating life and power.

MEMORIZE: *"Likewise the Spirit also helps in our weaknesses. For we do not know what we should pray for as we ought, but the Spirit Himself makes intercession for us with groanings which cannot be uttered. Now He who searches the hearts knows what the mind of the Spirit is, because He makes intercession for the saints according to the will of God."* (Romans 8:26-27)

Use the following lines to write out the scripture to help you commit it to memory.

_____

_____

_____

_____

_____

_____

_____

KEY TRUTH: The Holy Spirit is the leader and guide of your life and ministry of prayer in bringing man to God and God to man.

## YOUR RESPONSE:

This is how you can choose to live by the power of the Holy Spirit as you apply the truths from this lesson to your life.

- Daily submit your life and ministry of prayer to the leading, guiding and empowering of the Holy Spirit. As you begin your times of prayer in the language of the Holy Spirit, listen for what the Spirit will reveal as to how you are to pray in the understanding with understanding.

- Ask the Holy Spirit daily to reveal the will of God in every situation and come into agreement with it in faith.

- In seeking to pray according to the Word of God, listen for the Holy Spirit to give you specific scriptures to pray as you "unsheathe the sword of the Spirit" in Spirit-led, pinpoint accuracy.

- Everyday appropriate and activate the armor of God by always letting your prayer and supplication be in and by the power of the Holy Spirit.

## WRITTEN RESPONSE: LESSON REVIEW

Review each section from the lesson on the previous pages to fill in each blank below. This review will help to reinforce the truths from this lesson in your life.

1. The Holy Spirit is the _____ and _____ of your life and ministry of _____ in bringing _____ to _____ and _____ to _____.

2. Praying is doing the _____ of God to see the _____ of God _____ in the earth.

3. If the key to effective _____ is to _____ the _____ of God and come into _____ with it by faith, then we must _____ how to _____ the _____ of God.

4. We are called to "_____" the sword of the Spirit, which is the specific _____ _____ of God, _____ and _____ words of transformational _____ in prayer.

5. May we be found _____ rising in faith-_____, Spirit-_____ and Spirit-_____ prayer to see the _____ and the _____ of God _____ and _____ in all of its liberating _____ and _____.

**WRITTEN RESPONSE:** LIFE REFLECTION

Using the journaling section on the pages at the end of this lesson, write in your own words your responses to the following questions.

1. What have you learned and what has impacted you personally from this lesson?

2. In reading the scripture references in this lesson, what are you sensing and seeing the Holy Spirit highlight and reveal to you that will enable you to better live by the power of the Holy Spirit in everything?

3. As a disciple choosing to live by the power of the Holy Spirit, what steps of faith-filled obedience do you need to take to see what you have learned in this lesson become ongoing practices and patterns in your life?

*Journal*

*Journal*

# LESSON 5

## THE POWER OF THE
## HOLY SPIRIT IN PRAISE

## INTRODUCTION

❏ *Read Psalm 145:2; 1 Corinthians 14:15;*
  *Ephesians 5:18-20; Hebrews 13:15*

The Spirit-filled life is the praise-filled life. The Old and New Testaments are filled with examples of the Spirit of God coming upon people and empowering them for the ministry of praise. The Holy Spirit provides us with greater revelations of the Father and the Son and equips and empowers us to respond. The entire collection of the book of Psalms was written as men were moved by the Holy Spirit. (❏ Read Psalm 33:1; 43:1; 47:1; 63:1-5.) The Spirit of the LORD rested upon David and anointed him to become "the sweet psalmist of Israel." (❏ Read 2 Samuel 23:1-2.) The Spirit upon the prophet Isaiah enabled him to see exalted revelations of God and the appropriate praise responses. (❏ Read Isaiah 6:1-4; 12:1-6.) The Day of Pentecost was immediately marked by divine utterances of the wonderful works of God from the mouths of people freshly baptized and filled with the Holy Spirit. (❏ Read Acts 2:4-11.)

> *What we praise we will portray. What we behold we will become.*

What we praise we will portray. What we behold we will become. The Holy Spirit liberates us from rival affections so that we may exclusively behold Christ and be transformed into Christ's image from glory to glory.

(❏ Read 2 Corinthians 3:17-18.) It is the Spirit who anoints a new royal priesthood that we are a part of to proclaim the praises of Him who called us out of darkness and into His marvelous light. (❏ Read 1 Peter 2:4-9.)

## SPEAKING PRAISE

*Speaking praise* is the vocal declaration of the divine essence and grand exploits of God. Humanity is hardwired for praise. The terms for *praise* in the Bible have to do with celebration, admiration, and recognition. (❏ Read Psalm 66; Psalm 138.) The Bible's commands to admire and celebrate God are to be accompanied by clapping the hands, shouting, jumping, and rejoicing. (❏ Read Psalm 149; Psalm 150.) The people and things we admire the most are what we talk the most about. The ministry of praise is about using our words to put the focus and attention on the greatness of God's attributes and acts. Praise is vocal, passionate, purposeful and perpetual.

> *Speaking praise is the vocal declaration of the divine essence and grand exploits of God.*

Under the anointing of the Holy Spirit, King David wrote that he was committed to praise the name of God every day forever and ever. (❏ Read Psalm 145:2.) For David, the ministry of praise was not simply a once-a-week exercise for the gathering place with the saints. Praise was his personal, daily habit. David said what

Notes

he heard the Spirit speak to him concerning God which was then in his mouth and on his lips for everyone to hear. His commitment was to speak constant words of praise rather than praise that was intermittent or occasional. David's declaration was that praise was continually to be his devotion and his declaration. (❏ Read Psalm 34:1.)

The first sign of Holy Spirit baptism in the early church was divinely inspired words about the wonderful works of God. (❏ Read Acts 2:4-11.). These newly Spirit-baptized believers spoke words of grand praise as the Spirit gave them utterance. Jesus said that the Holy Spirit would glorify Him. (❏ Read John 16:14.) On the Day of Pentecost in an upper room 120 followers of Jesus experienced that very thing. The Holy Spirit who poured out heaven's glory on them released the words of God's glory through them as powerful, prophetic praise.

## GIVING THANKS

*Giving thanks* has to do with words offered from a grateful heart for God's gracious blessings. The most popular phrase for *giving thanks* in the Old Testament is "bless the LORD." It means ascribing words of gratitude to God as the Source of all blessings. Under the anointing of the Holy Spirit, King David said he not only committed himself to bless the LORD at all times, but that he would do so with all of his heart and soul. (❏ Read Psalm 103:1.) Jesus, the Anointed One, continually gave thanks to the Father in anticipation of the Father's miraculous works and in response to the Father's gracious provision. (❏ Read Matthew 11:25; 14:19; 26:26; John 11:41.) Paul told the Ephesians that a supernatural byproduct of continual Spirit fullness would be the giving of thanks to the Father for all things. (❏ Read Ephesians 5:20.) The Philippians and Colossians were exhorted to always give thanks in the midst of their praying. (❏ Read Philippians 4:6; Colossians 4:2.) Paul, a man greatly anointed by the Holy Spirit, considered constant rejoicing, ever-ready praying, and giving thanks to God in everything as keys to promoting the Holy Spirit's activity in the church, and not quenching (or extinguishing) it. (❏ Read 1 Thessalonians 5:16-19.)

> *Giving thanks has to do with words offered from a grateful heart for God's gracious blessings.*

## SINGING PSALMS, HYMNS, AND SPIRITUAL SONGS

*Singing* is putting words of praise and thanks into a vocal melody. Singing is not optional for the Spirit-empowered believer. The sons of Korah were inspired by the Spirit to command God's people to sing praises to God with understanding. (❏ Read Psalm 100:1-5.) The Psalms command us to make vocal melody concerning God's righteousness, the honor of God's name, His power and

His strength. (❏ Read Psalm 7:17; 21:13; 47:7; 66:1-4.)

Paul told the Ephesians that their continually being filled with the Holy Spirit would produce the singing of psalms, hymns, and spiritual songs. (❏ Read Ephesians 5:18-20.) *A psalm* is often regarded as singing words taken straight from Scripture. A hymn usually refers to a song based on the truths of Scripture. *A spiritual song* is a melody of spontaneous, Spirit-inspired words given to an individual at a given time. The Apostle Paul said that he prayed with the Spirit (in the spiritual language given to him by the Holy Spirit) and then prayed with the understanding (praying the revealed will of God in Paul's native tongue). (❏ Read 1 Corinthians 14:15.) He also said that he sang with the Spirit and sang with the understanding. According to the New Testament, spiritual songs arise from singing in our spiritual language and allowing the Holy Spirit to reveal a unique song of praise in our native tongue to lift up to God as well.

> *The Spirit is our ultimate worship leader in this life. He provides us with ever deepening revelation of the Father and the Son and equips and empowers us to respond in the most fitting way.*

There is a significant difference between praying in the

flesh (in our own strength and wisdom) and praying in the Spirit (by His strength and direction). There is also a significant difference between speaking praise, giving thanks, and singing unto God in our own strength and style, and doing so by the empowerment of the Holy Spirit. The Spirit is our ultimate worship leader in this life. He provides us with ever deepening revelation of the Father and the Son and equips and empowers us to respond in the most fitting way. (❑ Read John 4:23-24.)

MEMORIZE: *"Therefore by Him let us continually offer the sacrifice of praise to God, that is, the fruit of our lips, giving thanks to His name."* (Hebrews 13:15)

Use the following lines to write out the scripture to help you commit it to memory.

_____

_____

_____

_____

_____

_____

_____

KEY TRUTH: The Holy Spirit provides us with ever deepening revelation of the Father and the Son and equips and empowers us to respond in the most fitting way.

## YOUR RESPONSE:

This is how you can choose to live by the power of the Holy Spirit as you apply the truths from this lesson to your life.

- Ask the Holy Spirit to lead and empower you in speaking praise to the Father and the Son.

- Ask the Holy Spirit to lead and empower you to always recognize and give thanks for God's blessings.

- Ask the Holy Spirit to fill you and guide you in singing psalms and hymns to the Father and the Son.

- Spend time singing with the Spirit and intently listening for a spiritual song to lift up to the Father and the Son.

## WRITTEN RESPONSE: LESSON REVIEW

Review each section from the lesson on the previous pages to fill in each blank below. This review will help to reinforce the truths from this lesson in your life.

1. The Spirit-_____ life is the praise-_____ life.

2. What we _____ we will _____. What we _____ we will _____.

3. _____ _____ is the vocal _____ of the divine _____ and grand _____ of God.

4. _____ _____ has to do with words offered from a _____ heart for God's _____ blessings.

5. _____ is putting words of _____ and _____ into a vocal melody. _____ is not _____ for the Spirit-_____ believer.

**WRITTEN RESPONSE:** LIFE REFLECTION

Using the journaling section on the pages at the end of this lesson, write in your own words your responses to the following questions.

1. What have you learned and what has impacted you personally from this lesson?

2. In reading the scripture references in this lesson, what are you sensing and seeing the Holy Spirit highlight and reveal to you that will enable you to better live by the power of the Holy Spirit in everything?

3. As a disciple choosing to live by the power of the Holy Spirit, what steps of faith-filled obedience do you need to take to see what you have learned in this lesson become ongoing practices and patterns in your life?

*Journal*

*Journal*

# THE POWER OF THE HOLY SPIRIT'S GIFTS, PART 1

## INTRODUCTION

❑ *Read 1 Corinthians 12:7-11*

The gifts of the Holy Spirit are available to every born-again, Spirit-baptized and Spirit-filled believer. These gifts of divine grace give us the ability to engage in and accomplish the supernatural ministry of Jesus in the church and in the world.

The Holy Spirit uses each of us as He wills to be effective ministers of Christ's authority and power.

> *The gifts of the Holy Spirit are available to every born-again, Spirit-baptized and Spirit-filled believer.*

The word *gifts* has to do with the delegation and dispensation of God's grace to equip and empower followers of Jesus to continue His ministry in the earth. These gifts are like tools in a toolbox that the Holy Spirit places in our hands to help edify, encourage and equip others.

The Holy Spirit's gifts can be placed in three categories. First there are *revelation* gifts, which include the word of wisdom, the word of knowledge and discerning of spirits. These gifts enable you to *see* something that you could not see if God didn't reveal it. Then there are *power* gifts, which include the gift of faith, gifts of healings and working of miracles. These gifts enable you to *do* something that you could not do if God didn't give you the divine ability.

Lastly, there are *vocal* gifts, which include the gift of prophecy, different kinds of tongues and the interpretation of tongues. These gifts enable you to *say* something that you wouldn't be able to say without the Holy Spirit's enabling.

## THE WORD OF WISDOM

A *word of wisdom* is an inspired message that reveals God's plan for the wisest and most effective way to approach a given situation. There was a problem in the church in Jerusalem regarding whether Gentile believers would be required to be circumcised and live according to the law of Moses. The leaders in the church received divine wisdom on how to deal with this problem, granting spiritual liberty to Gentiles and releasing fresh spiritual life to the whole church. Everyone rejoiced at the anointed solution and strategy to the challenging issue they faced. (❏ Read Acts 15.)

*A word of wisdom is an inspired message that reveals God's plan for the wisest and most effective way to approach a given situation.*

## THE WORD OF KNOWLEDGE

A *word of knowledge* is an inspired message of knowledge concerning a person or situation that could only be

Notes

revealed by God. In the early days of the church, a couple named Ananias and Sapphira lied about an issue of property and profit. This threatened the purity and power that was present in the church. The Holy Spirit gave the Apostle Peter knowledge concerning their deception. The sin was revealed, judgment fell, and the church was struck with a fresh and new sense of godly fear and awe. This led to greater holiness in the church and many new believers were added to them. (❏ Read Acts 5:1-16.) Sometimes a word of knowledge is given to show someone that God knows exactly what his or her need is and to demonstrate God's willingness to meet that need.

> *A word of knowledge is an inspired message of knowledge concerning a person or situation that could only be revealed by God.*

## FAITH

A *gift of faith* is a supernatural confidence and trust that God is going to act in a powerful or miraculous way. One day Peter and John were going to the temple to pray. At the gate called Beautiful sat a man who had been lame from birth, begging for whatever people might give him. When Peter saw him, Peter was filled with faith. In the name of Jesus, he commanded the lame man to rise and walk. The man was immediately healed by God's miracle working power. (❏ Read Acts 3:1-16.) While every believer

A gift of faith is a supernatural confidence and trust that God is going to act in a powerful or miraculous way

is called to grow in faith in God's Word, will and ways day-by-day, there are times when the Holy Spirit grants a gift of faith that significantly adds to daily faith taking it to a new and more deeply dynamic level of miraculous potential.

## GIFTS OF HEALINGS

*Gifts of healings* are given to release Christ's power, causing people to be restored to health physically, mentally, emotionally and spiritually. There was a great move of God's Spirit in the city of Samaria under the ministry of Philip, an evangelist in the early church. The gospel was being preached, people were being saved and gifts of healings were being released in the lives of many who were physically broken and spiritually bound. (❏ Read Acts 8:4-8.) It is important to remember that no one has the gift of healing; it is the healing itself that is the gift, received and released through the hands of a Spirit-filled believer who

Gifts of healings are given to release Christ's power, causing people to be restored to health physically, mentally, emotionally and spiritually.

is submitted to the Spirit's empowering and enabling and desiring to be used to help and heal others.

## THE WORKING OF MIRACLES

A *miracle* is an event in which people or circumstances are unusually affected and changed in supernatural ways by God's power working through believers. The healing of the lame man at the Beautiful Gate is a clear example of a miracle. The power of God brought life and strength into a man's legs that were weak and withered from birth. He walked and leaped and praised God in the presence of many people. This sign and wonder was seen by all. (❏ Read Acts 3:1-10.) Even the religious leaders who were hostile to Jesus had to admit that this was a notable miracle—something that brought glory, honor and praise to Jesus. This miracle was followed by the ministry of declaring the message of God's good news of salvation in and through Christ Jesus. (❏ Read Acts 4:15-16.) Miracles are signs that make people wonder. They either precede and prove the gospel message before it is preached, or proceed and prove the gospel

> *A miracle is an event in which people or circumstances are unusually affected and changed in supernatural ways by God's power working through believers.*

message after it is preached. (❏ Read Mark 16:17-20.)

MEMORIZE: *"There are diversities of gifts, but the same Spirit. There are differences of ministries, but the same Lord. And there are diversities of activities, but it is the same God who works all in all."* (1 Corinthians 12:4-6)

Use the following lines to write out the scripture to help you commit it to memory.

_____

_____

_____

_____

_____

_____

KEY TRUTH: We have been given gifts of divine grace by the Holy Spirit to accomplish the supernatural ministry of Jesus in the world.

## YOUR RESPONSE:

This is how you can choose to live by the power of the Holy Spirit as you apply the truths from this lesson to your life.

- Spend time every day praying in the Spirit, asking the Holy Spirit to fill you freshly and to enable you to function effectively in His gifts of grace.

- Commit to walking and working in the supernatural power of God in the secret place, the gathering place and the public place.

- Let every relationship be infused with the person and power of the Holy Spirit to edify, encourage and equip those you seek to love and serve.

- Expect the preaching of the gospel to be preceded, proceeded and proved by the power of the gifts of the Holy Spirit.

## WRITTEN RESPONSE: LESSON REVIEW

Review each section from the lesson on the previous pages to fill in each blank below. This review will help to reinforce the truths from this lesson in your life.

1.  A _____ _____ _____ is an inspired _____ that _____ God's plan for the _____ and most _____ way to approach a given situation.

2.  A _____ _____ _____ is an inspired _____ of _____ concerning a _____ or _____ that could only be _____ by God.

3.  A _____ _____ _____ is a supernatural _____ and _____ that God is going to act in a _____ or _____ way.

4.  _____ _____ _____ are given to release Christ's _____, causing people to be restored to health _____, _____, _____ and _____.

5.  A _____ is an event in which _____ or _____ are unusually affected and changed in _____ ways by God's _____ working through _____.

**WRITTEN RESPONSE:** LIFE REFLECTION

Using the journaling section on the pages at the end of this lesson, write in your own words your responses to the following questions.

1. What have you learned and what has impacted you personally from this lesson?

2. In reading the scripture references in this lesson, what are you sensing and seeing the Holy Spirit highlight and reveal to you that will enable you to better live by the power of the Holy Spirit in everything?

3. As a disciple choosing to live by the power of the Holy Spirit, what steps of faith-filled obedience do you need to take to see what you have learned in this lesson become ongoing practices and patterns in your life?

*Journal*

*Journal*

# LESSON 7

# THE POWER OF THE HOLY SPIRIT'S GIFTS, PART 2

## INTRODUCTION

❏ *Read Matthew 10:1-8*

*Notes*

As stated in the last lesson, the gifts of the Holy Spirit are available to every born-again, Spirit-baptized and Spirit-filled believer. These gifts of divine grace give us the ability to engage in and accomplish the supernatural ministry of Jesus in the church and in the world. The Holy Spirit uses each of us as He wills to be effective ministers of Christ's authority and power.

Again, the word *gifts* has to do with the delegation and dispensation of God's grace to equip and empower followers of Jesus to continue His ministry in the earth. These gifts are like tools in a toolbox that the Holy Spirit places in our hands to help edify, encourage and equip others.

> *The Holy Spirit uses each of us as He wills to be effective ministers of Christ's authority and power.*

As a helpful reminder, the Holy Spirit's gifts can be placed in three categories. First there are revelation gifts, which include the word of wisdom, the word of knowledge and discerning of spirits. These gifts enable you to *see* something that you could not see if God didn't reveal it. Then there are power gifts, which include the gift of faith, gifts of healings and working of miracles. These gifts enable you to *do* something that you could not do if God didn't give you the divine ability. Lastly, there are vocal gifts, which include the gift of prophecy, different kinds of tongues and the interpretation of tongues. These gifts enable you to *say* something that you wouldn't be able to say without the Holy Spirit's enabling.

## PROPHECY

*Prophecy* is speaking forth a message from the Father or the Son for the church in order to edify, exhort or comfort His people. Prophecy can be the *foretelling* of some future event that helps people better prepare themselves for what God is about to do and how to better obey Him. Prophecy is also the *forthtelling* of a word which reveals the Lord's heart, purpose and plan for His people. On the Day of Pentecost, Peter preached and prophesied to the thousands of people gathered in Jerusalem. He explained that the outpouring of the Holy Spirit that day was a fulfillment of Joel's prophecy. (❑ Read Joel 2:28-32; Acts 2:17-21.) He also told them of things to come and how to respond to God's plans in order to receive God's promises. This word of prophecy served a dual purpose of forthtelling and foretelling, as the word opened their spiritual understanding to what was

> *Prophecy is speaking forth a message from the Father or the Son for the church in order to edify, exhort or comfort His people.*

*Notes* and what was to come. This word edified them (built them up), exhorted them (stirred them up), and comforted them (lifted them up). (❏ Read 1 Corinthians 14:3; Acts 2:1-42.)

## DISCERNING OF SPIRITS

*Discerning of spirits* is inspired understanding of whether an activity is of the Holy Spirit, the human spirit, or a demonic spirit. There was a slave girl following the Apostle Paul and declaring that he and his companions were servants of the Most High God. Even though her words were accurate, Paul discerned that she was possessed with a spirit of divination. She actually had the right words, but they were was spoken from a wrong spirit seeking to distract and confuse. Paul commanded the spirit to come out of her, and she

> *Discerning of spirits is inspired understanding of whether an activity is of the Holy Spirit, the human spirit, or a demonic spirit.*

was delivered. (❏ Read Acts 16:16-18.) Paul never allowed his discernment concerning the spiritual realm to grow dim or go dark. We must follow his example and never allow our discernment of the spiritual dimension to grow dim or go dark. The Holy Spirit sees to it that we can sense and see clearly enabling us to discern and determine the most appropriate course of action.

## DIFFERENT KINDS OF TONGUES

Speaking in *different kinds of tongues* is a Holy Spirit-given ability to speak in a language, of heaven or earth, which has not been learned by the speaker. On the Day of Pentecost, 120 people were filled with the Holy Spirit and spoke in languages they had never learned. People from around the world who were in Jerusalem for the feast heard these people praising God in their own language and dialect. It was a sign and wonder to them causing many to believe in the resurrected Jesus Christ. (❏ Read Acts 2:1-11.) The Apostle Paul told the Corinthian church that there was another kind of language that no one understands. It was a spiritual language that had to be interpreted by the Holy Spirit. Speaking in tongues as a gift of the Spirit is speaking a mystery and a message *from God to man*, being accompanied by the gift of the interpretation of tongues. This is different from the spiritual language that is to be used for prayer and praise, which is speaking a mystery and a message *from man to God*. (❏ Read 1 Corinthians 14:2-5.)

> *Speaking in different kinds of tongues is a Holy Spirit-given ability to speak in a language, of heaven or earth, which has not been learned by the speaker.*

# INTERPRETATION OF TONGUES

*Interpretation of tongues* is the Holy Spirit-given ability to speak in the language of the listeners the meaning of the prophetic message given in an unknown tongue. The Apostle Paul taught that prophecy was to be greatly desired because it brought divine understanding to the church and that spiritual language with interpretation was equivalent to prophecy. Again, a good way to look at the use of tongues or spiritual language is that praying and praising in tongues is speaking mysteries *to God*, and a message in a spiritual language with interpretation is speaking mysteries *from God*.
(❑ Read 1 Corinthians 14:5; 13, 26-28, 39.)

The Holy Spirit has come into our lives to fill us with the life of Jesus. The Holy Spirit has come to give us His gifts of divine revelation and power to obey Jesus and glorify Him in everything. These gifts enable us to enter into the same type of life-changing ministry as our Lord. We must not neglect nor refuse these gifts of grace. Rather, we should passionately desire the release of the power of the Holy Spirit's gifts. If we are open and willing, He will use us to minister powerfully,

> *Interpretation of tongues is the Holy Spirit-given ability to speak in the language of the listeners the meaning of the prophetic message given in an unknown tongue.*

both personally and corporately, to the needs of those we
are called to serve.

MEMORIZE: *"But the manifestation of the Spirit is given to each one for the profit of all:"* (1 Corinthians 12:7)

Use the following lines to write out the scripture to help you commit it to memory.

_____

_____

_____

_____

_____

_____

_____

KEY TRUTH: The Holy Spirit has come to give us His gifts of divine revelation and power to obey Jesus and glorify Him in everything.

## YOUR RESPONSE:

This is how you can choose to live by the power of the Holy Spirit as you apply the truths from this lesson to your life.

- Commit yourself to walking in the same power as Christ walked in.

- Surrender each new situation of your day to the leading and empowering of the Holy Spirit.

- Obediently respond to whatever gift or gifts He's distributing to you.

- Imitate and emulate those who walk in greater power, faith, and discernment than you do.

## WRITTEN RESPONSE: LESSON REVIEW

Review each section from the lesson on the previous pages to fill in each blank below. This review will help to reinforce the truths from this lesson in your life.

1. Again, the word _____ has to do with the _____ and _____ of God's grace to _____ and _____ followers of Jesus to continue His _____ in the earth.

2. _____ is speaking _____ a _____ from the Father or the Son for the church in order to _____, _____ or _____ His people.

3. _____ _____ _____ is inspired _____ of whether an activity is of the _____ Spirit, the _____ spirit, or a _____ spirit.

4. Speaking in _____ _____ _____ _____ is a Holy Spirit-given _____ to speak in a _____, of heaven or earth, which has _____ been _____ by the speaker.

5. _____ _____ _____ is the Holy Spirit-given _____ to speak in the _____ of the listeners the _____ of the prophetic _____ given in an _____ tongue.

**WRITTEN RESPONSE:** LIFE REFLECTION

Using the journaling section on the pages at the end of this lesson, write in your own words your responses to the following questions.

1.  What have you learned and what has impacted you personally from this lesson?

2.  In reading the scripture references in this lesson, what are you sensing and seeing the Holy Spirit highlight and reveal to you that will enable you to better live by the power of the Holy Spirit in everything?

3.  As a disciple choosing to live by the power of the Holy Spirit, what steps of faith-filled obedience do you need to take to see what you have learned in this lesson become ongoing practices and patterns in your life?

*Journal*

*Journal*

# LESSON 8

# THE POWER OF THE HOLY SPIRIT'S FRUIT, PART 1

## INTRODUCTION

❏ *Read Galatians 5:22-23; Ephesians 5:8-10*

The Holy Spirit comes to form the life and character of Christ in us. Christ's life and character in us is manifested as spiritual fruit that blesses and builds those we touch. This fruit is produced as we choose to remain in an intimate, loving and life-giving relationship with our Lord by the power of the Holy Spirit. This is what the Bible calls *abiding* in Christ. (❏ Read John 15:1-8.) So then, bearing spiritual fruit is the result of remaining in an abiding relationship with Jesus Christ through the person and power of the Holy Spirit at work in us.

> *... bearing spiritual fruit is the result of remaining in an abiding relationship with Jesus Christ through the person and power of the Holy Spirit at work in us.*

## THE FRUIT OF THE SPIRIT IS LOVE

*God's love in us is infinitely beyond the scope of human ability.* God's Word commands us to love with a love that is unceasing and never failing. In Greek, the word for this kind of love is the word *agape*. It could be described as *a love that does whatever it takes for as long as it takes*. (❏ Read 1 Corinthians 13:4-8.) The expression of this kind of love would be impossible in our own strength. But by the power of the Holy Spirit, we have an unending and inexhaustible flow of the supernatural love of God that enables us to love others constantly and continually.

*This love finds it's point of origin in the very heart of God.* The love that we are to walk in cannot be produced in the heart of man. It is produced in God's heart and poured into our hearts as we receive Jesus as Savior, Lord and King, and continue to abide in Him by His Spirit. (❏ Read Romans 5:5; 1 John 4:7-19.)

*Everything in our lives in Christ must be motivated and moved by God's love in us and through us.*

*God's love is clearly seen in the gift of His Son.* The Apostle John tells us that the manifestation or open display of the love of God can most clearly be seen in God sending His Son to sacrifice His life to pay for the sin of the world. God did this because of His infinite and undying love for all people. (❏ Read 1 John 4:9-10.)

*God's love in Christ Jesus through the power of the Holy Spirit is the primary and preeminent fruit from which all other aspects of spiritual fruit flow and grow.* The chief attribute of God is love. (❏ Read 1 John 4:8.) The controlling principle and practice of the church is love. (❏ Read 1 Corinthians 13:13.) Everything in our lives in

Christ must be motivated and moved by God's love in us and through us. This is what the Holy Spirit comes to provide and produce as the evidence that we are children of God our Father and followers of Jesus our Lord.

## THE FRUIT OF THE SPIRIT IS JOY

*Joy is delight and satisfaction in the human soul that grows out of an intimate relationship with the Lord Jesus.* It is a sense of gladness and well-being that becomes something too wonderful for words. (❑ Read 1 Peter 1:8.) This Spirit-supplied joy releases stability and strength for life and service. (❑ Read Nehemiah 8:10.) Joy is also the very atmosphere of God's kingdom *ever present* where Jesus is *very present*. (❑ Read Romans 14:17.)

*This joy is beyond circumstances.* Natural joy and happiness are based on happy events such as births, weddings or holidays. These things are wonderful and hold an important place in our lives. But life's circumstances are often trying and difficult and nothing in our lives is permanent. The supernatural joy of the Lord as a fruit of the Spirit's powerful work in our lives is always present

> *The supernatural joy of the Lord as a fruit of the Spirit's powerful work in our lives is always present regardless of our circumstances, delightful or difficult.*

regardless of our circumstances, delightful or difficult. In the Scriptures, Jesus' followers were always full of joy no matter what they faced. (❏ Read Acts 5:40-41; 16:22-25; Philippians 1:18.)

## THE FRUIT OF THE SPIRIT IS PEACE

*Spirit-supplied peace produces undisturbed composure, calm and contentment.* God's desire for us is to live without fear and anxiety. God's peace, produced by the Holy Spirit, supplies the inner serenity we need to stay anchored to God's promises. The Apostle Paul, though writing from prison, spoke of the great contentment and peace he experienced because of the strength and power of Christ through the Holy Spirit. (❏ Read Philippians 4:6-13.)

> God's peace, produced by the Holy Spirit, supplies the inner serenity we need to stay anchored to God's promises.

*Spirit-supplied peace produces peace with God, self and others.* We have peace with God because Jesus, through the Cross, put to death the power and penalty of sin that separated us from God. (❏ Read Colossians 1:20.) This supernatural peace with God now enables us to have peace with ourselves and to live in peace, harmony and unity with other believers, regardless of race, gender or any cultural or theological difference. (❏ Read Ephesians 2:14-18.)

## THE FRUIT OF THE SPIRIT IS LONGSUFFERING

*Longsuffering is the ability to patiently bear with a difficult person or situatio*n. God desires to empower us to help difficult people and to bring resolution and remedy in difficult situations. He, in fact, uses these people and situations to work depth and maturity in us. The longsuffering that comes by the power of the Holy Spirit within us gives us the grace we need to stand strong, stay strong and grow strong in the process. (❏ Read Colossians 3:12-13.)

*Longsuffering is the ability to wait patiently, faithfully and hopefully until God's will and good purpose are revealed.* God's plans are always ultimately good and fruitful. The Holy Spirit gives the strength to steadfastly endure until God's divine and desired outcome is accomplished. The Holy Spirit provides perseverance that produces proven character. This proven character then releases biblical hope—a settled confidence in a certain future in God through Jesus Christ by the Holy Spirit. (❏ Read Romans 5:1-5.)

> *The Holy Spirit gives the strength to steadfastly endure until God's divine and desired outcome is accomplished.*

# THE FRUIT OF THE SPIRIT IS KINDNESS

*Kindness is love and goodness in action.* It is the willingness to become involved in meeting the needs of others with love and grace, regardless of their response. (❏ Read Titus 3:4-5.) Reaching out to others to make every attempt to connect them with the love and kindness of God is a primary occupation for the follower of Jesus. The good news of the gospel and the good works of the bearer of the gospel must always go hand in hand.

*As we abide in Christ, remain freshly filled with the Holy Spirit and yield to His life and leading, we will see rivers of spiritual blessing flow in us, through us and out of us into the lives of others.*

*Kindness is a consistent and constant quality of a covenant-keeping God.* In both the Old and New Testaments God the Father is revealed as the One filled with lovingkindness for those He has created. (❏ Read Psalm 63:3-5.) When we extend Spirit-empowered and Spirit-supplied kindness to others, we imitate our Heavenly Father who does everything He can to reveal His heart of *tenacious tenderness* to any and all who will turn to Him.

*Kindness flows out of the riches of God's grace.* God extended His kindness to us by His grace in the lavishly generous gift of His Son, Christ Jesus. (❏ Read Ephesians 2:6-7.) Because of the person and power of the Holy Spirit in our lives, we have a rich repository of God's grace and goodness. We have an endless reserve to draw from in expressing God's love and kindness to others. As we abide in Christ, remain freshly filled with the Holy Spirit and yield to His life and leading, we will see *rivers* of spiritual blessing flow in us, through us and out of us into the lives of others. (❏ Read John 7:38-39.)

MEMORIZE: *"But the fruit of the Spirit is love, joy, peace, longsuffering, kindness, goodness, faithfulness, gentleness, self-control. Against such there is no law."* (Galatians 5:22-23)

Use the following lines to write out the scripture to help you commit it to memory.

_____

_____

_____

_____

_____

_____

_____

KEY TRUTH: The Holy Spirit comes to form the life and character of Christ in us. Christ's life and character in us is manifested as spiritual fruit that blesses and builds those we touch.

## OUR RESPONSE:

This is how you can choose to live by the power of the Holy Spirit as you apply the truths from this lesson to your life.

- Daily yield to the person and power of the Holy Spirit, asking Him to do an ever-deepening work of forming Christ in you and releasing His life and character through you.

- Recognize and respond to the reality that asking for a fresh filling of the Holy Spirit each day not only supplies the spiritual resources needed to minister the Holy Spirit's gifts but also to bear the Holy Spirit's fruit.

- Give attention to every interaction with others, monitoring and measuring whether the fruit of the Holy Spirit is evident and on display.

- Choose to deny the flesh and submit to the Holy Spirit's power for fruitful living moment by moment throughout the day.

## WRITTEN RESPONSE: LESSON REVIEW

Review each section from the lesson on the previous pages to fill in each blank below. This review will help to reinforce the truths from this lesson in your life.

1. God's _____ in Christ Jesus through the _____ of the Holy Spirit is the primary and preeminent _____ from which _____ other aspects of spiritual fruit _____ and _____.

2. _____ is _____ and _____ in the human soul that grows out of an _____ relationship with the Lord Jesus.

3. Spirit-supplied _____ produces undisturbed _____, _____ and _____.

4. _____ is the ability to wait _____, _____ and _____ until God's _____ and _____ _____ are revealed.

5. _____ is _____ and _____ in action. It is the _____ to become involved in meeting the _____ of others with _____ and _____, regardless of their _____.

## WRITTEN RESPONSE: LIFE REFLECTION

Using the journaling section on the pages at the end of this lesson, write in your own words your responses to the following questions.

1. What have you learned and what has impacted you personally from this lesson?

2. In reading the scripture references in this lesson, what are you sensing and seeing the Holy Spirit highlight and reveal to you that will enable you to better live by the power of the Holy Spirit in everything?

3. As a disciple choosing to live by the power of the Holy Spirit, what steps of faith-filled obedience do you need to take to see what you have learned in this lesson become ongoing practices and patterns in your life?

*Journal*

*Journal*

*Journal*

# THE POWER OF THE HOLY SPIRIT'S FRUIT, PART 2

## INTRODUCTION
❏ *Read Galatians 5:22-23; Ephesians 5:8-10*

As stated in the last lesson, the Holy Spirit comes to form the life and character of Christ in us. Christ's life and character in us are manifested as spiritual fruit that blesses and builds those we touch. This fruit is produced as we choose to remain in an intimate, loving and life-giving relationship with our Lord by the power of the Holy Spirit. This is what the Bible calls abiding in Christ. (❏ Read John 15:1-8.) Again, bearing spiritual fruit is the result of remaining in an *abiding* relationship with Jesus Christ through the person and power of the Holy Spirit at work in us.

> *Christ's life and character in us are manifested as spiritual fruit that blesses and builds those we touch.*

## THE FRUIT OF THE SPIRIT IS GOODNESS
*Goodness is love heaping blessings and benefits on others.* As an outgrowth of the Spirit and with God as our pattern, goodness will produce a life of generosity towards those around us. (❏ Read Psalm 107; Romans 2:4.) The divine fruit of *goodness* in Galatians 5:22 is a direct reference to the unchanging, unending goodness of God. One of Israel's favorite songs to sing to the LORD is found in 2 Chronicles 5:13, "For He is good, for His mercy endures forever." This

song in some form or variation is mentioned all throughout the Old Testament. God *is* good. Being good is who He is all the time and in every way. God does nothing, thinks nothing, says nothing except what is good and will produce good. God has always been good and will always be good.

*Spiritual goodness will produce practical results.* Scripture says that Barnabas was a good man. (❏ Read Acts 11:24.) We see the results of this goodness in his sacrificially meeting the needs of others. (❏ Read Acts 11:23-30.) Goodness is the divine quality of always thinking, saying, and doing what is good—just like God. Goodness is an unchanging state of thinking, saying, and doing what will produce good. This is what the Holy Spirit empowers us to do. He's the One who helps us to say and do nothing except what is good and will produce good. (❏ Read Ephesians 4:29.) He is the one who sees to it that God's goodness in Christ Jesus is manifested through us in generosity and consistency. (❏ Read Ephesians 2:10; Colossians 1:9-10.)

> *Goodness is the divine quality of always thinking, saying, and doing what is good— just like God.*

## THE FRUIT OF THE SPIRIT IS FAITHFULNESS

*Our faithfulness is founded and rooted in God's*

*faithfulness.* God's faithfulness to us is both the model and the means by which we are able to be faithful to Him and to others. (❏ Read Psalm 40:10; Lamentations 3:22-25.) Faithfulness is a confidence in God that produces a consistency of service. Those most confident in God become the most reliable Christians. God never fails. There has never been a time nor will there ever be a time when God will not come through on His word. Every promise He makes is His guarantee to make good on that promise. While on earth, Jesus was reliable and perfectly consistent. There was no cost He was unwilling to pay, no privilege He was unwilling to give up, and no suffering He was unwilling to endure to make good on God's promises. (❏ Read Hebrews 12:1-2.) He was faithful to the end and by His Spirit helps us to do the same.

*Faithfulness is submission to God in action.* True submission and obedience to God's Word, will and ways is demonstrated

> *The Spirit produces in us an ever-growing confidence in God that results in an ever-deepening consistency of service to God and others.*

by consistent faithfulness in whatever God has called us to. (❏ Read Hebrews 3:1-6.) Faithfulness has to do with quick and consistent obedience to God no matter what. One of the names ascribed to Jesus is "Faithful." (❏ Read Revelation 19:11.) Jesus was and is faithful to obey His

Father's will and to meet His people's needs. Through the Holy Spirit, this Man called "Faithful" lives in us. The Spirit produces in us an ever-growing confidence in God that results in an ever-deepening consistency of service to God and others.

## THE FRUIT OF THE SPIRIT IS GENTLENESS

*Gentleness is strength under restraint.* Gentleness and meekness go together. But meekness is not weakness. Jesus was strong in every way yet ministered in a sensitive gentleness to all He touched. (❏ Read Isaiah 40:11; Matthew 5:5; Matthew 11:28-30.) God only exerts the amount of strength that will help and bless someone. As a gentle and loving Father, He will only use His strength to secure and sustain, never to hurt or be harsh. Because God never uses His strength to hurt or be harsh, neither should we. Harshness hurts and hinders, while gentleness helps and heals. The Apostle Paul admonished the Philippians that the fruit of gentleness should be manifested to all. (❏ Philippians 4:5.) Gentleness should be a defining attribute of disciples and followers of Jesus. Gentleness is about saying the right words at the right time in the right way.

> *Gentleness should be a defining attribute of disciples and followers of Jesus.*

*The goal of gentleness is to bring about redemption and restoration.* This sensitive strength is to be used in a way where people receive the teaching and touch they need for growth, maturity and understanding. It is also used to bring loving correction in the lives of others. (❏ Read Galatians 6:1; Philippians 4:1-5.) The Spirit of Jesus daily enables us to speak and act in a way that redemptively ministers to others.

## THE FRUIT OF THE SPIRIT IS SELF-CONTROL

*Self-control is the ability to have power and governance over one's attitudes and actions by the power of the Holy Spirit.* The Spirit guides us and gives us the capacity to control and govern our thoughts and behavior under the Lordship of Jesus Christ. (❏ Read Galatians 5:24-25.) Through new birth in Christ, our desires change. Through the indwelling presence of the Holy Spirit, we begin to desire the things of God and are given an ability to conquer temptations to sin. The Apostle Paul wrote that by the Holy Spirit a new law of spiritual life is at work in us. (❏ Read Romans 7:21-8:2.) Yet, there are still desires in us for things that are not of God. Paul writes that this is a competing law that seeks to lead us back into sin and death. This is what is meant by

> *The fruit of self-control is the strength to refuse one thing and choose another.*

the word flesh. The flesh wants what is contrary to the Holy Spirit. The Holy Spirit and our new spiritual self want what is contrary to the *flesh*. (❏ Read Galatians 5:19-21.) This is where the *fruit of self-control* becomes essential to living in spiritual victory.

*Self-control is the ability to say "no" to all that God forbids and "yes" to all that He permits and ordains*. The ability to say "no" and "yes" by the Spirit is a major key in living out a successful and victorious Christian witness. (❏ Read 1 Corinthians 9:25-27; 2 Peter 1:5-8.) The word for *self-control* in the New Testament literally means to master something or bring something under your total authority. The fruit of self-control is the strength to refuse one thing and choose another. God doesn't "take control" of any person's life. What He does is lead us by the Holy Spirit to what is good and right and then give us the power to choose what is good by His grace. The ability to say "no" to all that God forbids and "yes" to all He permits and ordains for maximum blessing in life comes by the work of His Spirit in us and through us. (❏ Read 2 Peter 1:3-4.)

*Notes*

MEMORIZE: ..."as *His divine power has given to us all things that pertain to life and godliness, through the knowledge of Him who called us by glory and virtue, by which have been given to us exceedingly great and precious promises, that through these you may be partakers of the divine nature, having escaped the corruption that is in the world through lust.*" (2 Peter 1:3-4)

Use the following lines to write out the scripture to help you commit it to memory.

_____

_____

_____

_____

_____

_____

_____

KEY TRUTH: Bearing spiritual fruit is the result of remaining in an abiding relationship with Jesus Christ through the person and power of the Holy Spirit at work in us.

## YOUR RESPONSE:

This is how you can choose to live by the power of the Holy Spirit as you apply the truths from this lesson to your life.

- Ask the Holy Spirit to identify any inconsistencies and lack of integrity in your life. Repent and commit to walking in the Spirit, allowing Him to bear the fruit of unchanging goodness in every area of your life.

- Allow the Holy Spirit to bear in you a divine confidence in God that produces the same consistency of service to God and others that Jesus modeled.

- Ask the Holy Spirit to empower you to say the right words at the right time in the right way; allow Him to empower you to only display the right amount of strength that will serve and bless another.

- Ask the Holy Spirit to empower you to refuse the lusts of your flesh and choose the leading of His voice.

## WRITTEN RESPONSE: LESSON REVIEW

Review each section from the lesson on the previous pages to fill in each blank below. This review will help to reinforce the truths from this lesson in your life.

1. Again, bearing spiritual _____ is the result of remaining in an _____ relationship with Jesus Christ through the _____ and _____ of the Holy Spirit at _____ in us.

2. _____ is love heaping _____ and _____ on others. As an _____ of the Spirit and with God as our pattern, _____ will produce a life of _____ towards those around us.

3. _____ is _____ to God in _____. True _____ and _____ to God's Word, will and ways is demonstrated by consistent _____ in whatever God has called us to.

4. _____ is _____ under _____. Gentleness and meekness go together. But meekness is _____ _____. Jesus was _____ in every way yet _____ in a sensitive _____ to all He touched.

5. _____-_____ is the ability to have _____ and _____ over one's _____ and _____ by the power of the Holy Spirit.

**WRITTEN RESPONSE:** LIFE REFLECTION

Using the journaling section on the pages at the end of this lesson, write in your own words your responses to the following questions.

1. What have you learned and what has impacted you personally from this lesson?

2. In reading the scripture references in this lesson, what are you sensing and seeing the Holy Spirit highlight and reveal to you that will enable you to better live by the power of the Holy Spirit in everything?

3. As a disciple choosing to live by the power of the Holy Spirit, what steps of faith-filled obedience do you need to take to see what you have learned in this lesson become ongoing practices and patterns in your life?

*Journal*

*Journal*

# THE POWER OF THE HOLY SPIRIT'S SANCTIFICATION, PART 1

## INTRODUCTION

❏ *Read John 17:16-19*

*Notes*

The basic meaning of sanctification is *to set something apart for the use intended by the designer or creator*. In a biblical sense, things and people are sanctified when they are dedicated to and used for the purpose God the Designer and Creator intended. In the Scriptures, the word *sanctification* means *holiness*. To sanctify, then, means *to make holy*.

According to the Scriptures, the Holy Spirit comes into people's lives for the purpose of spiritual transformation and renovation that results in being conformed more and more into the glorious image of Jesus. (❏ Read 2 Thessalonians 2:13-14.) Also, sanctification produces outer separation and consecration. Sanctification then is an inner transformation and renovation that leads to an

> *Sanctification then is an inner transformation and renovation that leads to an outer separation and consecration.*

outer separation and consecration. This separation has to do with being separated from the world, separated to God, and separated for purpose. The Holy Spirit literally makes one holy as they receive God's gift of salvation and the baptism and filling with the Holy Spirit by grace through faith. By the same Spirit one is renewed and restored progressively, spirit, soul and body, being set apart increasingly for the divinely intended purposes and plans of God. (❑ Read 1 Thessalonians 5:23.) These purposes and plans always result in greater *internal* passion, purity and power that results in greater *external* passion, purity and power. (❑ Read 2 Corinthians 3:18.)

## SPIRITUAL TRANSFORMATION AND RENOVATION

The Holy Spirit's person and power comes into our lives to make us holy *from the inside out.* For many, holiness is trying to avoid things the Bible deems and describes as sinful and destructive. But true holiness is found in an inner change of attitudes, affections and appetites that are manifested in outer approval, attentions and actions. King David, later in his life, wrote to the young telling them that when they *loved what God loves, they would get what God gives*. (❑ Read Psalm 37:3-4.) The Holy Spirit comes to help produce an inner delight in the ways of God, which produces an inner desire for the ways of God. The result is a fully integrated life of devotion to the Word, will and ways of God that produces a life free of compromise and contradictions that which is

> *The Holy Spirit comes to help produce an inner delight in the ways of God, which produces an inner desire for the ways of God.*

deeply and simply satisfying. The Apostle Paul clearly states that sanctification is the eternal will of God for the life of every true believer in Christ. (❏ Read 1 Thessalonians 4:1-7.)

Before Christ, our lives are like a house that needs to be transformed and renovated, where rubbish is removed and beauty, order and true functionality is restored. A house is designed to be a safe, secure and sound place where people live, love and thrive. It is *sanctified* when that purpose is realized. When that purpose is compromised, transformation and renovation is needed to restore it to its originally intended purpose. And so it is with lives that are marred by sin – spiritual transformation and renovation must be worked out and brought to completion by the power of the Holy Spirit. (❏ Read Philippians 2:12-13.)

## SANCTIFIED IN OUR SPIRITS

The Apostle Paul says that it was and is God's purpose and plan in Christ Jesus to sanctify us completely in our spirit. This means that our spirits, which were dead toward God before conversion and new birth, are now made alive in Christ Jesus by the regenerating work of the Holy Spirit, to have clear, clean, holy and uncompromised fellowship with Him. (❏ Read Ephesians 2:1-7; Titus 3:5.) For our lives to be strong spiritually, we must wholeheartedly give ourselves to the ongoing inner work and witness of the Holy Spirit. This comes by submitting to the Lordship of

*For our lives to be strong spiritually, we must wholeheartedly give ourselves to the ongoing inner work and witness of the Holy Spirit.*

Christ, the power of the Holy Spirit, the authority and activity of the Scriptures and engaging in the spiritual disciplines of prayer, praise and meditation each and every day. Our spiritual lives are truly sanctified when we are fully devoted to what we were designed for—unbroken and uncompromised fellowship with God.

## SANCTIFIED IN OUR SOULS

The soul is made up of our mind, emotions and will. Each part of our soul was created and sanctified for specific purposes. This inner transformation and renovation that we have been looking at is directed toward us recovering all that was lost in the fall of Man and receiving a level of restoration that takes us on to unimagined heights of closeness with God and creativity through God.

Our minds were created to think God's thoughts, believe God's truth and see and imagine God's creative possibilities. The Holy Spirit comes into our lives to restore our minds and renew them ongoingly. (❏ Read Romans 12:1-2; Ephesians 4:20-23; Colossians 3:8-11.) As believers, we should be the clearest thinkers in the world, and we should be the cleanest thinkers in the world. There should be *holiness in our heads* as we allow the Holy Spirit to *make in our minds* what *makes up our minds*. The only thing that can compromise and corrupt this process is if we fill our minds with that which is unclean and unholy. This is why the Scriptures call and command us to set our mind on heavenly things. (❑ Read Colossians 3:1-4.)

Our emotions are ultimately informed and activated by our minds. If our minds are renewed, restored, and reoriented by the Word and the Spirit to think God's thoughts and believe God's truth, our emotions will

> *The soul is made up of our mind, emotions and will.*

be fed by this divine resource. How we feel is an accurate representation of our perception of reality. But reality must always be measured by what is true. Our feelings must line up with what is true in order for them to be truly sanctified or function according to their originally intended design. This is why it is so important that our affections are directed towards the things of the King and the kingdom. The Scripture tells us that we are not to love the things of the world—all of which are rooted in lust and pride. (❑ Read 1 John 2:15-17.) For when we love the world and cater to the flesh, we make room for the devil. But when we love the Word and walk by the person and power of the Holy Spirit, we make no room for the devil to deceive and destroy. Sanctified emotions are nourished by faith in what is truly sound.

Our will is focused and fixed by what is developed in our minds and emotions. If our minds and emotions are truly sanctified, our choices will be changed and conformed by the Holy Spirit and according to the life-giving commandments of God. Again, inner transformation and renovation will produce outer consecration to and cooperation with the purposes of God. It is such an exciting proposition to consider that the Holy Spirit desires to reside in us in order to transform us by His power and to conform us into the image and likeness of the Holy One, Jesus, our Sanctifying Savior.

## SANCTIFIED IN OUR BODIES

Our bodies are made to be instruments of righteousness and holiness. (❏ Read 1 Corinthians 6:12-20; 2 Corinthians 7:1; Romans 6:12-14.) When inner sanctification is established and ongoingly increasing in our spirit and soul, the body will naturally and supernaturally follow suit. As the body's appetites are re-set and reoriented

*When inner sanctification is established and ongoingly increasing in our spirit and soul, the body will naturally and supernaturally follow suit.*

according to the things of God, it is a relatively simple matter to avoid that which keeps us from achieving our true potential in Christ. Simply put: When we are filled and satisfied with all that God has to offer, we are not hungry for all that the world, the flesh and the devil have to offer. This is such a key and often missing principle in the life of the believer: inner sanctifying transformation and renovation by the person and the power of the Holy Spirit produces outer separation and consecration for the works of God.

MEMORIZE: *"Now may the God of peace Himself sanctify you completely; and may your whole spirit, soul, and body be preserved blameless at the coming of our Lord Jesus Christ."* (1 Thessalonians 5:23)

Use the following lines to write out the scripture to help you commit it to memory.

_____

_____

_____

_____

_____

_____

_____

KEY TRUTH: The Holy Spirit, by His person and power, comes into our lives to do a deep and divine work of sanctification which produces complete inner transformation and renovation.

## YOUR RESPONSE:

This is how you can choose to live by the power of the Holy Spirit as you apply the truths from this lesson to your life.

- Freshly yield to the Holy Spirit to bring transformation and renovation into your life, spirit, soul and body, asking Him to reveal areas of compromise and corruption.

- List areas where you believe you have engaged in simply trying to avoid sinful and harmful things rather than allowing the Holy Spirit to alter your appetites so that your actions correspond to righteous affections.

- Pay attention to how former temptations wane and weaken in light of your fresh commitment to inner sanctification, transformation and renovation.

- As you journal, keep a careful record of your spiritual growth and development of being transformed and conformed into the image of Christ.

## WRITTEN RESPONSE: LESSON REVIEW

Review each section from the lesson on the previous pages to fill in each blank below. This review will help to reinforce the truths from this lesson in your life.

1. According to the _____, the Holy Spirit comes into people's _____ for the purpose of _____ _____ and _____ that results in being _____ more and more into the glorious _____ of Jesus.

2. The Holy Spirit's _____ and _____ comes into our lives to make us _____ *from the* _____ _____.

3. Our spiritual _____ are truly _____ when we are fully _____ to what we were _____ for—_____ and _____ fellowship with God.

4. Again, inner _____ and _____ will produce outer _____ to and _____ with the purposes of God.

5. When inner _____ is established and ongoingly increasing in our _____ and _____, the _____ will _____ and _____ follow suit.

## WRITTEN RESPONSE: LIFE REFLECTION

Using the journaling section on the pages at the end of this lesson, write in your own words your responses to the following questions.

1. What have you learned and what has impacted you personally from this lesson?

2. In reading the scripture references in this lesson, what are you sensing and seeing the Holy Spirit highlight and reveal to you that will enable you to better live by the power of the Holy Spirit in everything?

3. As a disciple choosing to live by the power of the Holy Spirit, what steps of faith-filled obedience do you need to take to see what you have learned in this lesson become ongoing practices and patterns in your life?

*Journal*

*Journal*

*Journal*

# THE POWER OF THE HOLY SPIRIT'S SANCTIFICATION, PART 2

## INTRODUCTION

❏ *Read 2 Corinthians 6:11-7:1*

*Notes*

Again, the basic meaning of sanctification is to *set something apart for the use intended by the designer or creator*. In a biblical sense, things and people are sanctified when they are dedicated to and used for the purpose God the Designer and Creator intended. In the Scriptures, the word *sanctification* means *holiness*. To sanctify, then, means to *make holy*.

As we stated, in the Scriptures the Holy Spirit comes into people's lives for the purpose of spiritual transformation and renovation that results in being conformed more and more into the glorious image of Jesus. (❏ Read 2 Thessalonians 2:13-14.) Also, sanctification produces outer separation and consecration. Sanctification then is an inner transformation and renovation that leads to an outer separation and consecration. This separation has to do with being *separated from the world, separated to God, and separated for purpose.* The Holy Spirit literally makes one holy as they receive God's gift of salvation and the

> *... the Holy Spirit comes into people's lives for the purpose of spiritual transformation and renovation that results in being conformed more and more into the glorious image of Jesus.*

baptism and filling with the Holy Spirit by grace through faith. By the same Spirit, one is renewed and restored progressively, spirit, soul and body, being set apart increasingly for the divinely intended purposes and plans of God. (❏ Read 1 Thessalonians 5:23.) These purposes and plans always result in greater *internal* passion, purity and power that results in greater *external* passion, purity and power. (❏ Read 2 Corinthians 3:18.)

## SEPARATED FROM THE WORLD

The Apostle John says all that is in the world is the lust of the eyes, the lust of the flesh, and the pride of life. He says the world and every lust in it are passing away. He explains that a person cannot love the world and love God.

> *Everything in the world is rooted in lust and pride. Everything in the kingdom is rooted in love and humility.*

To love God is to hate the world's system. The Father isn't a part of anything in the world's system. While the world and its lusts are passing away, John says that those who do the will of God will remain forever. (❏ Read 1 John 2:15-17.) This raises an important question: how does someone go from loving the world to loving God? Loving God is possible through the power of the Holy Spirit's sanctification. The Holy Spirit illuminates our hearts and minds to recognize what the world's system really are. Before we knew Christ, we lived in and for the world. In Christ, filled with His Spirit, we are taken out of the world's system and transferred into the kingdom of God. Everything in the world is rooted in lust and pride. Everything in the kingdom is rooted in love and humility. (❏ Read Colossians 1:13.) God lusts for nothing and has no pride. The Holy Spirit of God empowers and guides us out of thinking, talking, and acting in lust and pride like the world.

Whatever a disciple might lose or leave behind in the world in order to follow Jesus is nothing compared to what he gains. The things of this world (power, pleasure, the pursuit of wealth, etc.) look like good things that should be desired. Yet, the ruler of this world and the things he offers only lead to deception and destruction. (❏ Read John 10:10; 2 Corinthians 4:3-4.) A disciple doesn't become clear about the lethal and corrupting power of the world on his own. A disciple doesn't see the world's system for what it is simply by looking at the world's system. The key is to first look to Jesus and what He truly provides and then look at the world and what it falsely promises to provide. The apostles gladly left the world and all it offered *because they were looking at and to Jesus*. The Holy Spirit continually reveals Christ to a disciple and as a result, the disciple sees the world more accurately by comparison. When fellowship and partnership with the Father and the Son are compared to fellowship and partnership with the world, the better choice is made crystal clear. As we look daily to the Holy Spirit to grace us and to guide us He continues to provide the clarity that we need.

## SEPARATED TO GOD

The Holy Spirit always separates a disciple from one thing in order to set that disciple apart for something better. The ultimate reason for which the Holy Spirit separates someone from the world is for God Himself. God says that being separate from the world leads to being received by God as our Father. Being separated from the world is so God may walk among us. (❏ Read 2 Corinthians 6:16-17.) Paul calls an intimate walk with our Heavenly Father a promise to be deeply desired. (❏ Read 2 Corinthians 7:1.) But this promise is conditional.

*The primary reward of holiness is God.*

There are things we must do in order to receive and walk in this promise. Paul tells us that honoring God with worshipful reverence is key. Paul writes that believers are to cleanse their lives. The word in this verse for *cleanse* has to do with making something clean, removing stains, purifying from wickedness, and dedicating something to a holy purpose. Paul is saying that an intimate walk with God as Father is a promise for those who allow the Holy Spirit to continually remove from their lives anything unclean and continually dedicate themselves to a life of holiness.

Notes

The primary reward of holiness is God. Any sanctifying work of the Holy Spirit—whatever He might remove—has deeper fellowship with God in view. Inner spiritual sanctification resulting in outer physical sanctification will always produce greater intimacy with God.

## SEPARATED FOR PURPOSE

There is great work to be done with God and He wants us to join Him in that work. The Holy Spirit is sanctifying a holy people for holy purpose. Paul told Titus that denying ungodliness and worldly lust isn't an end in and of itself. He wrote that living righteously in this present age isn't an end in and of itself. He emphasized that Jesus was purifying a people who were zealous to do good works. (❑ Read Titus 2:11-14.) The word *zealous* in this verse means to burn in your soul with passion to do what you were born to do. Separated for purpose means that we join God in the works that we were created for.

> The Holy Spirit is sanctifying a holy people for holy purpose.

Jesus lived a life being sanctified for a holy purpose. He was offered everything the ruler of this world's system could offer. (❑ Read Matthew 4:1-11.) He left it all behind to lay hold of the great work His Father had set Him apart for. (❑ Read John 5:17-19.) He modeled for us that living in the purposes of God is a continual process of leaving behind and letting go of all that isn't of God. Often times what the Spirit is removing is not necessarily wrong, just wrong for what He has planned for us. The writer of Hebrews tells us that we are to lay aside *every weight*. (❏ Read Hebrews 12:1.) The word *weight* in this verse has to do with things that don't fit in a person's life or things that would hinder their progress. The Holy Spirit will remove what doesn't fit into God's current plans for us. He will also remove anything that weighs us down, slows us down, and keeps us from the good works God has prepared for us. (❏ Read Ephesians 2:10.)

MEMORIZE: *"Since you have purified your souls in obeying the truth through the Spirit in sincere love of the brethren, love one another fervently with a pure heart,"* (1 Peter 1:22)

Use the following lines to write out the scripture to help you commit it to memory.

_____

_____

_____

_____

_____

_____

_____

KEY TRUTH: Sanctification is an inner transformation and renovation that leads to an outer separation and consecration.

## YOUR RESPONSE:

This is how you can choose to live by the power of the Holy Spirit as you apply the truths from this lesson to your life.

- To the degree the Holy Spirit reveals worldliness in you, confess and repent of lust and pride in your life.

- Ask the Holy Spirit to show what He presently wants to separate you from.

- Allow the Holy Spirit to show you how He wants to make you closer with the Father and the Son.

- Ask the Holy Spirit to reveal the good works and purpose for which He is setting you apart in this season of your life.

## WRITTEN RESPONSE: LESSON REVIEW

Review each section from the lesson on the previous pages to fill in each blank below. This review will help to reinforce the truths from this lesson in your life.

1. In a _____ sense, things and people are _____ when they are _____ to and used for the _____ God the Designer and Creator _____.

2. _____ then is an inner _____ and _____ that leads to an outer _____ and _____.

3. Whatever a _____ might lose or leave behind in the _____ in order to _____ Jesus is nothing _____ to what he _____.

4. Inner _____ sanctification resulting in outer _____ sanctification will always produce _____ _____ with God.

5. The Holy Spirit is _____ a holy _____ for holy _____.

**WRITTEN RESPONSE:** LIFE REFLECTION

Using the journaling section on the pages at the end of this lesson, write in your own words your responses to the following questions.

1. What have you learned and what has impacted you personally from this lesson?

2. In reading the scripture references in this lesson, what are you sensing and seeing the Holy Spirit highlight and reveal to you that will enable you to better live by the power of the Holy Spirit in everything?

3. As a disciple choosing to live by the power of the Holy Spirit, what steps of faith-filled obedience do you need to take to see what you have learned in this lesson become ongoing practices and patterns in your life?

*Journal*

*Journal*

# LESSON 12

## LIVING BY THE POWER OF THE HOLY SPIRIT: THE CHOICE IS NOW YOURS

## INTRODUCTION

❏ *Read Galatians 5:16-25*

We began this resource by stating that living by the leading and power of the Holy Spirit enables us to live a life of fellowship, fullness and freedom. Once saved and baptized and filled with the Holy Spirit, we are invited and called by God to abide in the Spirit moment by moment and day by day. We are called not to live in our own strength but by the power and strength of God's Spirit. We are beckoned to allow the Holy Spirit to be our constant companion and helper, leading us into the will of God the Father and Jesus the Son and giving us the spiritual guidance and strength to see it come to pass. This is the way chosen for us by God the Father and Jesus the Son. So, will you live by your own strength and resources endeavoring to accomplish divine purposes through human means? Or, will you live and embrace the walk, the way and the work of the Spirit? *The choice is now yours.*

> *We are called not to live in our own strength, but by the power and strength of God's Spirit.*

## THE WALK IN THE SPIRIT

We have established that walking in the Spirit involves submitting to the *person, purpose and power* of the Holy Spirit. The Holy Spirit is the presence of the Father and the

*Notes*

170

Son in us, helping and guiding us to discover the Father's and the Son's will and purpose by divine wisdom and power. (❑ Read John 14:16; 15:26; 1 John 4:4.) Walking in the Holy Spirit is a partnership between the Holy Spirit and us. We yield to Him in faith and obedience and He supplies everything we need to be fruitful believers and ministers. He leads us as we study God's Word, giving us revelation and insight—eternal truth to learn from and live by. (❑ Read John 16:13-15.) He helps us in our human weaknesses to know how to pray and what to pray. (❑ Read Romans 8:26-28.) Paul told the Ephesian church that they would understand the power of this kind of living. In so doing they would find themselves strengthened by the mighty power of the Holy Spirit in them, rooted and grounded, full and satisfied in the love of Christ and the knowledge of His will for them. (❑ Read Ephesians 3:14-21.)

*By walking in the Spirit, we partner with the Lord Jesus in what He is doing around the corner and around the world, across the street and across the waters.*

It is no wonder we are called to "Walk in the Spirit." (❑ Read Romans 8:1-4.) It is the only truly wise and wonderful way to live. By walking in the Spirit, we partner with the Lord Jesus in what He is doing around the corner and around the world, across the street and across the waters. Our eyes are opened to see what He intends to do in our lives and times and how He intends on accomplishing it by His Spirit. So, will you walk your own way, creating your own path according to your own will and desires? Or, will you order your steps and walk the path of purpose and power provided by the Holy Spirit? *The choice is now yours.*

## THE WAY OF THE SPIRIT

We have made clear that the way of the Spirit is about a new kind of living. It is the way of abundant and glorious liberty. (❏ Read John 10:10; Romans 7:4-6.) The Holy Spirit desires to set us free from trying to do what is spiritually right in our own strength. He comes to set us free from the penalty, power, guilt and shame of sin. Sin no longer has dominion over us. (❏ Read Romans 6:11-14.) We are now free to serve and obey God on His terms according to the truth and direction of His Word and the leading and life of His Spirit. As we abide in Him and trust His strength, we have the supernatural ability to live for Jesus and obey Him in everything. This provides us with a life of high purpose and

*We are now free to serve and obey God on His terms according to the truth and direction of His Word and the leading and life of His Spirit.*

deep and abiding joy. So, will you live on your own terms, striving in your own strength to build a life that is full and rich? Or, will you live the new, glorious and abundant life that is according to the way designed and destined by God Almighty? The choice is now yours.

## THE WORK OF THE SPIRIT

We have stated that the work the Holy Spirit desires to accomplish in us is a work of *purity, passion and power*. Remember, He is called the *Holy Spirit*. He brings the purity of God's presence and character into our lives so that we can receive and reflect the glory of His holiness in the earth. (❏ Read 1 Peter 1:16.) This is not self-righteousness. In fact, it is the very opposite; it is the very righteousness of Christ received and released in us and through us by His Spirit.

> *... the work that the Holy Spirit desires to accomplish in us is a work of purity, passion and power.*

The Spirit also produces in us a deep, abiding passion to love Jesus supremely and seek to please Him everything. Paul told the Philippians that both the desire to fulfill God's will and the dynamic power to fulfill His will was the result of God's Spirit living within us. (❏ Read Philippians 2:12-13.) God in us by the Holy Spirit has come to see the full work of salvation in spirit, soul

*Notes*

and body become a blessed reality. This work in us then becomes the work through us that touches and transforms every life we encounter.

Remember the following truths concerning the work of the Holy Spirit in us:

- He makes us spiritually new. (❑ Read Titus 3:5.)

- He fills and empowers us to minister the life of Jesus. (❑ Read Acts 2:33.)

- He is the presence of the Father and the Son in us. (❑ Read John 14:15-18.)

- He produces the fruit of godly life and character in us. (❑ Read Galatians 5:22-23.)

- He leads and guides us into the perfect will of God on a daily basis. (❑ Read John 16:13-14.)

- He satisfies the deepest needs of our lives. (❑ Read John 7:37-39.)

- He fills us with the love of God. (❑ Read Romans 5:5.)

- He gives us supernatural gifts and abilities. (❑ Read 1 Corinthians 12:11.)

- He helps us pray with precision and power. (❑ Read Romans 8:26-28.)

- He opens our eyes to understand spiritual things. (❑ Read 1 Corinthians 2:9-16.)

- He produces unity with other believers, so we can live in peace and love. (❑ Read Ephesians 4:3-4.)

- He supplies the breakthrough power of the kingdom of God to overcome all the power of the kingdom of demonic darkness. (❑ Read Matthew 12:28.)

According to the Scriptures, living by the power of the Holy Spirit is the walk, the way and the work chosen for you by God the Father and Jesus the Son. If you will say yes to God's walk, way and work, you will find that living by the person and the power of the Holy Spirit in everything is the most fulfilling and exciting way to spend the days, months and years of one's lifetime. Engaging in this way of living will provide a life truly worth living. So, will you live below the divine purposes and privileges gained for you by the Lord Jesus? Or, will you embrace fully these divine purposes and privileges, living by the by the power of the Holy Spirit every moment of every day? The choice is now yours.

*According to the Scriptures, living by the power of the Holy Spirit is the walk, the way and the work chosen for you by God the Father and Jesus the Son.*

MEMORIZE: *"If we live in the Spirit, let us also walk in the Spirit."* (Galatians 5:25)

Use the following lines to write out the scripture to help you commit it to memory.

_____

_____

_____

_____

_____

_____

KEY TRUTH: Living by the leading and the power of the Holy Spirit enables us to live with fellowship, fullness and freedom.

## YOUR RESPONSE:

This is how you can choose to live by the power of the Holy Spirit as you apply the truths from this lesson to your life.

- Ask the Holy Spirit to reveal any area of your life where you have not fully submitted to Him, His purpose, and His power.

- Ask the Holy Spirit to reveal any area of your life where you are relying on your own strength instead of Him.

- Ask the Holy Spirit to reveal any area of your life where you are not allowing Him to work in you and through you.

- Take time to repent in the areas revealed to you above and make a fresh commitment to live by the power of the Holy Spirit each and every day.

## WRITTEN RESPONSE: LESSON REVIEW

Review each section from the lesson on the previous pages to fill in each blank below. This review will help to reinforce the truths from this lesson in your life.

1. We are _____ not to _____ in our own _____, but by the _____ and _____ of God's Spirit.

2. We are beckoned to _____ the Holy Spirit to be our _____ _____ and _____, leading us into the _____ of God the Father and Jesus the Son and giving us the _____ _____ and _____ to see it come to pass.

3. _____ in the Holy Spirit is a _____ between the _____ _____ and _____.

4. As we _____ in Him and _____ His strength, we have the _____ ability to _____ for Jesus and _____ Him in everything.

5. According to the _____, living by the _____ of the Holy Spirit is the _____, the _____ and the _____ chosen for _____ by God the Father and Jesus the Son.

**WRITTEN RESPONSE:** LIFE REFLECTION

Using the journaling section on the pages at the end of this lesson, write in your own words your responses to the following questions.

1. What have you learned and what has impacted you personally from this lesson?

2. In reading the scripture references in this lesson, what are you sensing and seeing the Holy Spirit highlight and reveal to you that will enable you to better live by the power of the Holy Spirit in everything?

3. As a disciple choosing to live by the power of the Holy Spirit, what steps of faith-filled obedience do you need to take to see what you have learned in this lesson become ongoing practices and patterns in your life?

*Journal*

*Journal*

*Journal*

*Journal*

*Journal*

*Journal*

*Journal*

*Journal*

*Journal*

*Journal*

*Journal*

Made in the USA
Columbia, SC
22 September 2019